ANGELS
&
SMUGGLERS
Journey Beyond Man's Authority

by Alyce Mann & Jimi Miller

A LIFE BOOK

Published by Life Books
          P.O. Box 719
          Uhrichsville, OH 44683

Printed in the United States of America.

Contents

Some of the characters, locations, and incidents have been altered to protect the innocent victims of cruel governments as well as the ministry that takes place on their behalf.

Acknowledgments

I would like to thank first of all the Lord Jesus Christ for the inspiration of the Holy Spirit. He who makes all things possible.

A special thank you to my husband, Charlie, who gave consistently of his time, talent, and energy in creating the manuscript. His friendship and support have become a mainstay in my life for which I am very appreciative.

Many hours at the computer also meant many hours away from my family. I applaud their patience and sweet release which made it possible for me to pursue God's calling.

Charlie and I both extend our heartfelt gratitude to Brother Andrew, whose steadfast service to the suffering church has given us a wonderful role model, one for which we have never had to apologize. Following in his footsteps has poised quite a challenge, a challenge that changed our lives forever.

My thanks to Pastor Michael MacIntosh who shared the truth of God with me. He set my feet on a firm foundation.

Dick Burow, Margie Johnson, Gloria Duncan, and Shana Fimbres also offered their support. Fortunately for me, their words of encouragement and good counsel came when I needed it the most.

Many thanks to the folks at Life Books, Ellen Caughey, Rebecca Germany, and Sue Gowins, to name but a few who worked on the final manuscript. Especially, Stephen Reginald, Vice President Editorial, for his professional assistance and guidance.

Finally, "We know that you have a choice in air travel," to quote one of the major carriers. Of course, I realize that the same is true in the world of literature. So a sincere thank you to you, the reader, for taking the time to learn about the suffering church. May your life be richer and your walk with the Savior closer because of it.

Foreword

One of the most common comments I used to hear, when I just began to relate my adventures behind the Iron Curtain to the American Christian public, was "OK, Andrew, that's all right for you as a Dutchman, you can do that, but we, Americans, cannot do that."

That was always the most devastating reaction I could get. My whole message consisted in not only telling about the fate of the persecuted church in the Communist-held countries, but also to get the church in the free countries into action and making them do what I was doing. So that more people would witness the persecution, get the burden for them, begin to pray, go and supply their needs. All this was possible and I knew it. After all, God is the same, isn't He? And nowhere, is there any Scripture verse that would indicate that Jesus is the same, yesterday, for all of us; today, only for the Dutch, and maybe tomorrow, for the Americans. No, He is the same, and is only one Body, one faith, one baptism, one Lord, and His Name is Jesus.

Lest I start preaching now, let me tell you how delighted I am with this book which shows you that the God Who saw me through, called me, protected me, did the miracles, gave the vision, blinded border guards' eyes, brought me miraculously in touch with those that were to receive my encouragement, that God is still the same for—not just those in this story—but for every American and whatever nationality. If we only dare to step out and let God do the walking through us.

This book delights me more than most of the books I have

read in my lifetime, because this is one of my dreams come true. Already as a missionary, I am extremely happy, because I have seen my big dreams come true: the Iron Curtain breaking down, the Wall disappearing and the many other problems solved—and in the wake of it, new problems coming into existence, but all of this is only a further challenge to all of us.

I have seen all this and now I see American people dedicated to Jesus and to the ministry to the Body of Christ and they go and it is an expansion of my own work, my vision and my own life. This is what God called me to with that word that still rings in my ear. I heard Him say it in July 1955 on my very first journey in Eastern Europe: "Awake, and strengthen what remains, which is at the point of death." (Rev. 3:2) "Awake," that means, I have to wake up. And when I wake up, I speak. And when I speak, I speak for those who cannot speak.

Now, others are waking up. As you read this charming book, you will fall in love with those that the book describes; the ones that God loves, the Body of Christ that needs our attention, our encouragement and everything we can give her, so that it will not disappear because of persecution, opposition and cruel oppressive regimes.

God has a call on all of us, as Christian soldiers. We must obey and start marching! So, as you read, say: "God, here am I. If you can do it through me, do it! But here am I."

God bless you as you read this fantastic book.

Your

Brother Andrew

1

America the Beautiful

It started in 1989 during January, when Charlie and I could no longer resist the prompting of the Holy Spirit. After two years of experiencing His loving persuasion, we finally decided to give in and agreed to go. Having caught the vision, we firmed up our plans to smuggle Bibles behind two invisible, very formidable walls, the East-European Iron Curtain and the Bamboo Curtain of China.

We occasionally harbored some reluctance toward the idea: To our way of thinking, there were more than enough needs to fill and problems to solve right here at home in the good old USA. Still, Matthew and Mark both record in their Gospels that the Lord Jesus Christ requires believers to take the Good News into all the world. We understood that more and more as our day of departure neared. Nevertheless, we watched in disbelief how opposition to the same Gospel continued to spread across our country. Many subtle questions lingered deep within our spirits. *Did God have more than one purpose for sending us on the journey? Was there a hidden message, some warning we were to bring back to America?* If so, what it might be, we could not imagine.

My husband Charlie is tall, dark and handsome with a wonderful face. Depending on what he wears, he could pass for a *paisano,* a *sabra,* or a member of Russian royalty. When he speaks, one would mistake him for a college professor which he is not. Charlie is a self-taught genius.

In 1985, we were living in San Diego, California, when we heard about a free, fried-chicken dinner sponsored by a mission organization at a local Denny's Restaurant. We liked chicken, we liked Denny's, and we liked free. Missionaries fascinated us, especially those courageous souls who smuggled Bibles. After a short discussion of the pros and cons, we decided to attend. Neither Charlie nor I knew much about the dark, shadowy world of atheistic communism, but we did understand that everyone everywhere needed the Word of God, especially in countries where it was forbidden literature.

When we arrived at the restaurant, there were still quite a few empty seats. Interest in the plight of overseas Christians was clearly somewhat limited. The meal was adequate—pretty much what we expected—but we had not come only for the food or only to listen. No, there was a hidden reason, one that at the time even we did not understand. There was no way for us to know or even to guess what God had planned for us in the future.

As soon as everyone had finished eating, the waiters cleared the tables leaving only the coffee cups and water glasses. Then, a regional representative of the mission stood up behind the podium and pinged on a glass with a spoon. When the general hubbub died down, he welcomed us, thanked everyone for coming, then introduced the main speaker, Peter Ming, an underground-church coworker who had barely escaped with his life from the People's Republic of (Red) China.

Brother Ming's manner was shy, his voice gentle, but his smile was bright and friendly. Behind his dark eyes lay the hidden secrets of "a persecuted people." At first, his words were difficult to understand. Realizing that it might be a problem for us, he apologized for his poor English. Eventually, as the audience adjusted, a holy hush came over the room.

Brother Ming brought greetings from the persecuted underground Church in China to the free Church in America. With heartrending emotion, he described the false imprisonments, the beatings, starvation, torture and overall brutality prevalent in his country. Still, he assured us that God was also working in China. In spite of constant suffering, the faithful believers numbered in the millions with new converts being added daily. To their government's frustration, no amount of persecution or oppression could stop the expansion of the Lord's harvest while the number of underground churches continued to multiply.

I thought, *Persecution? Oppression? Do I even begin to understand the implications of those words? What if I was denied my right to think, to make my own choices or decisions without government approval? Could I live like that? Could Charlie?* I glanced over at Charlie. He was fully absorbed by Peter Ming's words, obviously captivated by his transparent humility.

Brother Ming's narrow eyes became mere slits as he continued. "Christians in China are told by the authorities to believe in God, but act otherwise. In other words, we must keep our faith to ourselves and not honor His Commandments." He paused while his penetrating eyes took in his entire audience. "This is the only condition in my country under which my personal freedom is guaranteed. More and more frequently, the devil's messengers come to me saying, 'Go ahead, you can reject God's Commandments without rejecting God.' But, my friends, we know that is not true. Rejecting God begins with rejecting His Commandments. They amount to the same thing." Then his voice became strong and even more determined than before, when he said, "One of my brethren was told at his trial that he could believe in God and live according to the Bible in heaven, but not in China. Yet he answered the authorities strongly, 'If I do not live according to the Bible on earth, I will not go to heaven.'"

As I sat there next to Charlie, listening to the frail, brave Chinese Christian man plead for Bibles, for couriers and for prayers in behalf of China, the thought came to my mind, *How shallow is the outward expression of my own faith!*

Charlie remained motionless. The compelling message had touched him deeply. Then Brother Ming's final words were spoken with such intense passion that they cut my heart like a surgeon's scalpel: "If it ever comes to this, I will kiss the rope that hangs me, but I will never deny my Lord!"

Goose bumps swarmed across my arms while my seat felt like it had caught fire. I recognized the chill as a response to Peter Ming's words and the heat as conviction from the Holy Spirit. Until then, the most intense persecution I ever suffered as a Christian was an occasional snide remark about my faith in Jesus by my coworkers. But, forced to choose between life without Him, or death? *Could I? Would I? What kind of life would that be!*

An anointed silence swept over the souls gathered there in the dining room, one of those unexplainable, undeniable moments when time stands still while the people experience a supernatural touch from the Master. Not until the host returned to the microphone and began speaking did the overpowering trance throughout the room lift.

The mission desperately sought couriers to deliver Bibles, people to become "Bridge Builders," spokespersons to fill the gap between the Church in America and the Church behind the Iron and Bamboo Curtains. But it was the closing statement that kept repeating itself over and over in my mind:

Smuggling can be a difficult and challenging experience but if God is calling you, you will never rest until you go.

How true a statement it was, we would find out later.

As the crowd began to disperse, Charlie and I both sensed the Spirit of God urging us to become involved. It was then, after a quick pragmatic discussion, we concluded (in agreement with our carnal natures) that we were not cut out for it. We counted three obvious, legitimate, inarguable reasons that confirmed our decision:

1. With heavy schedules at home and at work, we were already too busy, and could not commit to any more assignments.

2. People like us don't go: We send money to preachers and missionaries who are paid to meet such needs.

3. There was plenty of rescue work to do right here in our own hometown in America.

The banquet room was almost empty when we stopped at the book table. Charlie wandered off to talk to someone he thought he recognized, leaving me standing there alone. I stared blindly at the brochures and books, keenly aware of a fierce battle raging between my willing spirit and my weak flesh. I kept thinking, *Alyce, if you wait until you feel like doing something of eternal value, you probably never will.*

"All right!" I mumbled, answering my own thoughts aloud. "I'll pray about it. Maybe at a more convenient time . . . ." Somehow those words sounded familiar and rang hollow. Translated they meant, "God, go away and leave me alone." As a diversion, I picked up a book and read the back cover:

A THANK-YOU LETTER TO CHINA'S COURIERS

Thanks our Heavenly Father who really listens to our prayer and touch the three of you to bring us the most wonderful gift in the World. On receiving, none of our brothers and sisters stopped praising and thanks our Heavenly Father. Some shed their tears continuously. Some cannot fall asleep the whole night but praising the Lord all the time. Some even forget their meals but keep on reading. All of them said, it is really the most precious thing among valuables. Because of this, we can only thanks our Father's love and grace. On the other hand we have to thanks you for accomplishing God's will, look down on yourselves, neglect the difficulties and send the precious gift from thousands of miles away. May Our Heavenly Father reward you Himself.

Therefore to him that knoweth to do good, and doeth it not, to him it is sin. (James 4:17)

How could I even suspect that God was also dealing with my husband in the same way? By the time he returned, my struggle had already transformed itself into words. Unable to conceal my inner turmoil, I blurted out, "Charlie, what should we do about this?"

My husband, who is not given to impulsive behavior, surprised me when he answered without any hesitation, "Hm, funny you should ask because I've been asking myself the same question. Still I thought we agreed this is not our type of ministry. But then, you know, why should we each have two Bibles when other believers have none? Doesn't seem right, does it?"

"No, it doesn't," I sighed with a little flood of relief.

When Charlie turned to face me, I could tell he was reconsidering. "I know we don't have to understand God's will to obey it. At the same time, there are hundreds of other causes needing support, right?"

"Right!" I agreed. "But, Charlie, what about this·one?"

"Well, it certainly strikes straight to the heart."

I nodded my agreement. We were wavering. There were dozens of worthy causes already petitioning us for support. We decided not to sign up as Bible couriers, but we did subscribe to the mission's newsletter and tape ministry. And, for the next two years, we sent money. We also became busier than ever in our church. We started by helping to feed the homeless, cooking in the church kitchen, collecting clothes for the poor, giving presents to needy kids at Christmas, increasing our charitable giving all around. Somehow, it wasn't enough.

On a quiet Tuesday evening during the fall of 1988, Charlie and I were sprawled across the living room carpet in the comfort and safety of our home in sunny California. We were listening to a cassette tape, an anointed message by Brother Andrew that spanned several years and thousands of miles. The ministries need had not changed. On the tape Andrew was pleading for someone—anyone—to take Bibles to the brothers and sisters in communist countries. And when we heard his words, "Someone needs to go. Why not you?," they pierced our souls.

Charlie and I stared at each other. Us, Lord? *Yes!* We both heard the inaudible answer. What supernatural force had broken through to our hearts? The tone of Andrew's voice? His sincerity? His charisma? Or had we both received a direct challenge from God?

For a moment, I was speechless, closing my eyes to keep my thoughts to myself: *No, Andrew, not me! I'm not even remotely courageous. Charlie maybe, but me? I don't smuggle Bibles. I send money. I'll send more! Okay, Lord?*

Evidently, my vision of God was too small for the assignment. Not that it mattered, because neither God nor Charlie were listening to my arguments conjured up on the spur of the moment. Brother Andrew continued to suggest that we stretch ourselves far beyond anything we ever believed possible. But how? How else but by going!

He closed his message with a chilling reference to crossing the borders: "I can promise to get you into those countries," he said, "but I cannot promise to get you back out. Our Lord only said, 'Go ye!' Didn't He? He never said that you would return."

I gulped. My heart began pounding. Surely, God did not expect Charlie and me to leave our familiar surroundings for parts unknown? I shook my head no, of course not. Then I had a second thought. *What if He did intend to use us? Gadzooks!* I took a deep breath and closed my eyes, then resolved that if that was His will, He would perform a miracle and convince me.

Days, weeks and months passed as He stirred our hearts with agonizing speculations. *What about His myriad of children deprived of His thoughts, His promises, His love and His power?* The question tormented our minds during our quiet moments. Jesus had placed His hand firmly on our lives.

By January, Charlie and I finally agreed we could no longer resist the Holy Spirit's prompting. Now we decided to take action on behalf of those caught in the grip of brutal government control and persecution. We must help Christians unable to speak for themselves. We must.

For us, the Suffering Church had come to represent a gaping wound in Christ's broken body. To minister to them was to express our love for Jesus, believing that in God's eyes the two acts were inseparable. Do we amputate or ignore an injured hand? No. We nurse it back to health until it is completely healed. The metaphor of the injured hand became very real to us. God had inspired us in such an undeniable way that Charlie and I both knew we had to help with the healing.

Even so, our wise pastor counseled us specifically about the absolute reality of spiritual warfare. He said, "Everything might be running smoothly when suddenly all kinds of opposition could come against you, vicious as well as subtle. At that point, one of two things will happen: either your fantasy of a romantic worldwide ministry will disintegrate into a nightmare or you'll remember that, no matter what circumstances Satan stirs up for you, God is still in control. Keep that always in mind: It's His ministry, not yours. He is Lord!"

The miracle occurred. We had received the guidance that we had prayed for. Only one problem remained. Our going would put Charlie's government job at risk. Neither of us wanted that, but we could not shake Brother Andrew's challenge or God's inspiration. With His words permeating our every thought, like Isaiah, we finally surrendered: "Here am I: send me."

We said it aloud together and immediately experienced God's blanket of supernatural peace. But apparently His peace was limited to Charlie and me. Almost everything I tackled at the office suddenly became a big issue. And, without exception, our friends expressed uneasy feelings about our plans.

Even my normally calm and confident mother panicked: "Where are you going? For how long? When will you return? Can you leave a phone number?"

No one understood that we were simply two obedient, devout cowards. It was for love of Jesus and submission to His will that we had agreed to go. Even admitting that, we still convinced no one. As far as they all were concerned, we were pursuing a grand folly.

Once our preparations were under way, everything moved smoothly. Too smoothly? People continued to be leery and to warn us about getting ourselves into trouble. But in spite of their well intentioned persistence, by the time we left for the airport Sunday morning in a rented car, our hearts were brimming with enthusiasm and confidence. We would soar with the eagles.

Charlie and I made record time on the hundred mile drive from our home in San Diego to the Los Angeles airport. We were even running slightly ahead of schedule when I dropped Charlie and our mountain of luggage off at the curb. Perhaps, we had over prepared by packing so many things: water pick, iron, photography magazines included. I smiled inwardly while my husband stood waiting in front of the Royal Dutch Airline (KLM) departure entrance as I pulled away enroute to the car rental office.

It wasn't until I pulled into a parking spot and turned off the engine that I suddenly remembered separating the first set of our tickets, those from Los Angeles to London, from the rest and putting them—where? In my purse? I could not remember. Frantically, I explored every compartment but came up empty-handed. "Jesus, please tell me that I haven't lost them," I stammered, struck by a rush of panic-packed adrenaline.

My hands shook as I searched through all our travel papers, reading them aloud to myself: international drivers' licenses, maps, instructions, passports, traveler's checks, tickets from London to. . . .

It was no use: The tickets for the first leg of our journey were simply not there. Somehow in all the last minute confusion I had misplaced them. Maybe, by some chance Charlie had picked them up; that was my only hope.

In desperation, I prayed, *Dear God, please don't forsake us now.*

I bolted out of the car, raced inside the office and rudely thrust the rental contract at the nearest agent. He finished his scribbling and I ran for the commuter bus. There was no time to lose. I had to make it or be stranded waiting for the next one. Fortunately, I was the last one on before the door closed. The bouncy ride made me nauseous so I kept swallowing hard to choke back the threatening acid in my throat.

After what felt like forever, the driver stopped directly across from Charlie. "You have the tickets, right?" I shouted to him from a few feet away.

"No," he said, looking at me puzzled. "I don't have them. You have them. You put them all together with the. . . . Is this a joke? You don't have them?"

"I don't! Oh, Charlie, I separated the first batch out so we could...I don't remember why. Dear, God, what are we going to do? Why do I always mess up everything? Why is nothing ever easy?"

"Never mind, Chop; stop beating yourself." Charlie always caught my attention by using my nickname. "You don't always mess up everything. This could happen to anyone—maybe. Don't worry, it's not over yet. We still have an hour-and-a-half before we board. You sit over there on the bench and think while I go to check on something."

He helped me carry the suitcases over and I flopped down on the seat still feeling shaky. I exhaled loudly watching him blend into the crowd. He quickly disappeared and I was alone. I closed my eyes and sat perfectly still thinking as hard as I could.

In my mind, I retraced all my steps from the moment that I took the tickets out of the folder. I knew I had planned to check them for some very good reason. Then, for some unfathomable other reason, I carefully replaced all the tickets except the ones to London, which I put—where?

2
Farewell to Freedom

It was nobody's fault but mine. Charlie and I had only covered the first hundred miles on our Bible smuggling adventure with Christ before we faced our first formidable roadblock. I had inadvertently left part of our super cheap round-the-world tickets at home.

Time was working against us. It was already two-thirty and our flight, the only daily KLM flight from Los Angeles to London to Amsterdam was scheduled to take off at 4:00 p.m. Unfortunately, the plane would leave with or without us.

"What can we do?" I asked Charlie after he returned from his first unsuccessful attempt at trying to resolve our dilemma. I gathered we were both bewildered when he answered me with a ponderous stare.

Since neither of us knew what else to do we decided to wait in line hoping that maybe a Customer Service agent might know how to solve our problem. The noisy crowd moved slowly only a few feet at a time which made me more and more fidgety.

At last, it was our turn and we stepped up in front of the counter. Quickly, urgently we began to explain our plight to the young man named Allan who admittedly seemed very sympathetic. Allan listened attentively to our plea for help only there was nothing he could do without the original tickets. And no matter what, there were simply no standby seats available on another flight until Wednesday.

With our situation worsening I complained to Charlie and whoever else might over hear. "This is not like me, I know better. I should have written 'Tickets' at the top of my list."

Charlie didn't answer me but I was sure I heard a breathy voice whisper, "You should give up and go home." Flustered, I spun around. Who said that, I wondered without recognizing any of the strangers nearby or the people in line.

"No. We won't," I said sharply after realizing the confusion and discouragement as tools of the devil.

Charlie looked surprised. "No, we won't what?"

I grimaced. "Never mind."

The two people behind us gave us a peculiar look and I could tell they were becoming restless and irritated by the delay. They were making me nervous. When Charlie noticed them, he tugged the sleeve of my jacket to move me aside before I embarrassed us any further.

We were stuck and I felt sick. The spiritual stakes were high because so many others were depending on us. The extent of my blunder stretched across the Atlantic and into Asia where hundreds of believers were waiting to receive copies of the Bible, the same Bibles we should be delivering. Someone else, if there was anyone else, would have to meet their need. Now it seemed as though our trip was ending before it even began.

"It's all my fault. Because of my blunder . . ."

Charlie interrupted. "Come on, quit it. Self-recrimination won't help. There must be something we can do. We need a plan."

He was right, of course, but I was at a loss.

We tramped back to the bench with our pile of luggage and I collapsed. Charlie remained standing, still seeming relatively cool and unruffled. He suggested, "Suppose I phone our travel agent. Perhaps, he can do something."

"It's Sunday and they're closed," I reminded him. "Besides, we don't have another eighteen hundred dollars for more tickets." My chin trembled but I knew Charlie didn't want me to cry. It wouldn't help anyway.

He glanced down at me. "No standby till Wednesday, is that what he said?"

"That's what he said," I sighed, feeling guilty purposely avoiding any eye contact.

"Well I guess if we can't get there, we can't get there." Charlie chewed on his lower lip and shook his head. I knew he was disgusted with me only was too nice to say so. "Come on Chop, let's go. We should go home, make some calls and try to void the other tickets while we can still collect a refund. Come on. It's only a trip. We'll live through it."

"I don't blame you for being angry," I said sheepishly, blinking back the tears.

"I'm not angry, I'm just . . ." His voice trailed off as he headed toward the water fountain leaving me sitting there alone. He finished taking a drink then walked around the corner. I felt deserted.

God, why would You choose us, especially me, for this gigantic undertaking? How did I manage to blow it before we even started?

No response. Then suddenly I thought I remembered where the tickets were. It was only a strong suspicion and I still couldn't be sure but now at least there was hope.

Charlie came back grinning and purring like a cat. "Good news," he exclaimed. "British Airways has a few seats open on their flight to London that has been delayed until six o'clock. The tickets must be at home somewhere and if you can remember where, maybe Bobby can bring them to us in time. The KLM manager said he would still be here to endorse them over to British Air. There's a chance we can make it. What do you think?"

"It's worth a try because you're right, I think I know where I left the tickets. A hundred miles is a long way, but . . ." I jumped to my feet and handed him all our other papers for safekeeping. "Here, you keep these. I'll call Bobby." I took off running through the terminal to locate a telephone. Now, if only our dear friend Bobby, our house sitter, is home to answer the phone.

My hand trembled as I dialed and prayed, *Please God, please let Bobby be there*. I closed my eyes and held my breath through seven rings. Finally, after the eighth ring, Bobby picked up. "You won't believe this Bobby but I think I left our tickets on the tan filing cabinet. Check and see, okay?"

"Alyce? Is that you? Are you kidding? Okay, hold on."

I heard only silence in the background until Bobby returned to the phone. "I'm holding two KLM tickets to London in my hand," he said.

"Thank God," I exclaimed.

Bobby continued "Alyce, is that what you wanted to know?"

"Yes. Can you bring them to us immediately if not sooner? We will meet you in front of the KLM entrance at LAX."

"I'll do my best," he added swiftly.

"Please hurry." I replaced the receiver and checked my watch, ten minutes after three. Traffic would be heavy. Is this what Pastor meant by spiritual warfare? *Lord are You really in control?*

"Bobby found the tickets and he's on his way," I announced to Charlie as I trotted back to where he was waiting somewhat patiently.

"Good I guess. I only hope it's not too late," he muttered. He stood up and shrugged his wide shoulders. "We're in for a long wait so I'm going for coffee. You coming or should I bring you a cup?"

At that moment more than anything I wanted to be alone. "No thanks, I'm not in the mood for anything, I'll stay here." I answered him feigning a smile.

Charlie disappeared and I hauled our luggage to a deserted area near the windows. I needed a private spot where I could seek the Father's face.

I was sitting quietly when for some reason, I remembered Moses and his prayer of intercession. I began to mimic his reasoning with God. After all, our defeat would create an embarrassing situation for Him. When cynics heard that we had failed, would they not ask arrogantly, "Where is their God?"

Lord, if You don't help us, won't Satan claim a victory? You tell us to feed Your sheep. Doesn't that mean to give them Your Word? Your wonderful Word is a powerful Love Letter that provides comfort, encouragement and guidance. Without it, we cannot carry on in this world.

I was deep in prayer when I suddenly discerned that the "accuser of the brethren" had come upon the scene. He reminded me how weak I was, how ungodly my imagination, how rebellious my attitudes. So I reminded him that the blood of Jesus Christ had already cleansed me of my sinful nature and that my faith in His atonement remained firm. I clenched my fist and lashed back at him in defiance: "The LORD rebuke you, Satan!"

He fled at the authority of God's Word and again I took hold of my Savior's unseen hand. I needed His strength to press on.

My personal time with the Savior passed quickly and before I knew it Charlie returned with a luggage cart. We loaded it and went out to the curb to watch for Bobby's red Cougar convertible. Neither Charlie nor I had very much to say. Prayer seemed much more important at the moment. Eventually, I spotted

Bobby's car heading up the ramp and checked my watch, 5:55 already. We sighed in relief as he pulled to a stop in front of us.

If God was truly in control, we needed two more miracles. One that would give us enough time to make the flight and the other to work out the public relations problem. And our luggage still had to be checked.

"Traffic was terrible," he said as if he should apologize. He held the precious tickets out the window looking worn-out and disheveled.

Charlie grabbed them out of his hand and said. "Listen, thanks a million, pal."

We both gave Bobby quick hugs over the car door then ran back inside. I struggled to keep up with my husband's long strides as we raced over to find the KLM manager. Without his endorsement, British Air could not honor the tickets.

Fortunately, we reached the counter as he emerged from the back area. He saw us and hurried over having already taken his pen out of his shirt pocket. Charlie handed him our papers and he opened the folder. We had not noticed the two words boldly stamped across the first page before: "NOT ENDORS-ABLE"

I withered. Now what?

The manager hesitated for a second and I thought I would faint. "I'm not supposed to do this," he said and crossed out the words, "but I will anyway." He finished initialing the page then returned them to Charlie.

"God bless you," my words blurted out surprising all three of us. Charlie thanked him and we ran across the lobby to British Air. Between gasps, I fought to hold back my emotions. Would we be too late? *Jesus, help us and make our feet like hinds' feet.*

By the time we arrived at the British Air ticket counter the line had vanished. Only one agent remained. We feared that the inactivity might be a bad omen until she flashed us a reassuring smile. Charlie quickly handed her our paperwork and she removed her copies, tagged our bags then placed them on the moving belt. We were still out of breath and panting but relieved to see them go.

"You're very lucky," she said straightening up to face us. "We've had another flight delay so your luggage might even arrive with you. Go to Gate 8 and hurry." It wasn't the moment to say so, however luck had nothing to do with it.

Holding our passes in one hand and our carryon luggage in the other we started running toward the boarding area. We cut in front of the people already standing in line and barged our way through security. Terribly inconsiderate but sorry, we were rushing.

The airline agent at the gate quickly ripped off the stubs and we ran down the corridor into the plane. After receiving a few peculiar looks from the other passengers we collapsed into the two remaining aisle seats as the flight attendant closed the hatch door.

Charlie reached across the aisle and squeezed my hand, then squeezed it again harder. His reassuring touch opened the floodgates and tears of relief flowed down my cheeks. I pulled tissue after tissue from my pocket to blot the embarrassing moisture. Secretly, I hoped no one noticed the big wet splotches on my blouse and jeans. If anyone did, they didn't seem to care.

Exhausted by the trauma, I leaned my head back, closed my eyes and blew the damp, dangling strands of hair off my face. What a bizarre beginning to our spiritual adventure.

I waited until we were airborne before digging my Bible out of my carryon stuffed under the seat in front of me. As the pages fell open, my eyes were drawn to the Scripture I needed most to see—the words of Jesus, "Never will I leave you; never will I forsake you." *Lord, please write that message on my heart so I never, ever forget it.*

As soon as I recovered from the ticket trauma I began to see some humor in our situation. This was Charlie's one and only vacation for the year. *Whose idea was this anyway?*

Foolish question. We knew Who wanted the Bibles distributed. Certainly not the world. Not our flesh and not the devil. It was God's idea. A matter of life or death for many: spiritual life or death and physical life or death in some cases. Even though our journey might involve some pretty terrifying twists and comical turns, it was still God's idea — an idea we had the privilege to share.

Then I felt a hand on my shoulder and glanced up into the gentle brown eyes of a young flight attendant. "Would you like dinner?" she asked politely.

"No, thank you anyway," I smiled in response.

After she handed Charlie his tray I turned sideways in my seat. I wanted to weigh today's frantic events against tomorrow's questions. *Jesus, whatever happens, You will stay with us, won't you?*

We dozed and chatted and dozed again and eventually the wheels of the jumbo jet touched down at Heathrow Airport just outside London. Now we had a forty minute layover before our commuter flight departed for Amsterdam. Fortunately, we located a currency exchange nearby where Charlie traded a few American dollars for a handful of British coins. A call to our contact person at the mission in Zwolle, Holland, to confirm that we were en route seemed appropriate. How convenient to find a telephone booth opposite the money exchange.

"Strange looking phone," I commented about the oversized, canary-colored instrument attached to the wall.

Charlie mumbled something unintelligible to me while attempting to decode the posted instructions for placing an overseas call. My Charlie, who can fix anything and could probably make a computer sing our national anthem, did not understand the directions. After a few minutes of indecision, I maneuvered him out of the way and pressed "O" for Operator.

"I want to place a call to Holland," I shouted in competition with the static of a bad connection. "Can you help me?"

"Yes indeed," she replied in a charming British accent. She told me the exact amount of money to be deposited in pounds, shillings, and pence. Her voice sounded sophisticated and ladylike reminding me of the distinguished Margaret Thatcher. My voice in contrast sounded earthy, street bred, twangy New Yorkese sprinkled with Jewish clichés.

Charlie stared blankly at the coins in his hand. "How much? Is this enough?"

I shrugged and remarked to the operator, "We don't know how many there are of what we have here."

I could hear the smile in her voice. "Drop your coins in the slot and I'll count them for you." Evidently, we weren't the first uneducated foreigners she had dealt with sight unseen.

I dropped and she counted. We were short. "What should we do?" I asked her.

"Shall I hold until you get some more money exchanged?"

"I don't think we have time since our flight is scheduled to leave shortly." Unbelievable, another quandary.

"Really? Where are you off to?"

"We're from San Diego, California, on our way to Amsterdam," I made an earnest effort not to sound anxious.

"You don't say. What an interesting coincidence. It's such a small world. Would you believe that I have a sister who lives in San Diego? Maybe you know her? Evelyn Jones?"

"No. Sorry, I don't." I rolled my eyes at Charlie who was watching me intently.

"Oh too bad. Dear me, poor old Evelyn," she continued. "I tried to warn her but she simply wouldn't listen. You know how it is between relatives sometimes. Anyway, she planned to marry an American sailor stationed there until she found out in the nick of time what I had been trying to tell her all along that . . ."

By now Charlie was glaring.

What could I do? I didn't want to be rude and just hang up. She chatted on and on until the pressure finally convinced me that I had to say something, "Sorry to interrupt you, but we have to . . ."

"Hold on dearie," she answered flippantly. "I almost have you through. All right, there it is. I'll connect you now. Have a nice trip."

"Hooray!" I muttered quietly.

Seconds later, an answering machine with a Dutch recording picked up the phone. Obviously, everyone had already left for the day. Even so, Charlie thought it would be wise to leave a message. I handed him the receiver and just as he was about to speak the line went dead. He was disconnected. Exasperated, we simply looked at each other while listening to the dial tone. I felt numb. Why wasn't anything ever easy? Was the entire trip going to be just one blind alley after another?

Happily, we caught our next flight without incident and the hop linking Heathrow with Amsterdam's Schiphol International Airport sped by quickly. Our baggage, on the other hand would not arrive until two hours later on the next plane from London. Why were we not surprised?

In an attempt to work the cramps out of my legs, I began a public regimen of squats and stretches until the expression on my husband's face sent a silent but loud message. It wasn't my intention to embarrass either of us so I stopped in favor of a more appropriate time and less conspicuous place. Charlie pointed to a row of empty benches setting over against a wall and suggested that we try to get some sleep. Sleep. The word sent a thrill of expectation all through my aching body.

Getting comfortable on the cold plastic cushions proved to

be impossible. I covered my head with my denim jacket in a futile attempt to muffle the blaring irregular announcements from the paging system. No use. As soon as one announcement ended I tensed up for the next one.

Finally, I gave up the pursuit of physical comfort and sat up. I reached for my Bible and the spiritual comfort tucked within the pages. I flipped to my record of answered prayers written in back. A smile spread across my face as I scanned though my notes, so many living witnesses and demonstrations of my Heavenly Father's love. God is good, Jesus is alive and generous with His mercy.

I took out my pen and recorded the chain of yesterday's miracles attached to the forgotten tickets. How unworthy and highly privileged I felt to serve the God Who is greater than any situation or circumstance, including all my shortcomings and deficiencies.

It was close to nine o'clock before our baggage arrived intact and we left the airport terminal for the short walk across the parking lot to the train station. By then we were both punchy from jet lag and lack of sleep.

At long last, the lemon-colored train rumbled down the tracks to transport us to Zwolle. The tiny village in the reclaimed outlands of Holland was our destination.

I started to crack a senseless joke until I caught a glimpse of my exhausted husband staggering down the platform. He was struggling with our huge suitcases, a heavy carryon and his bulky camera bag. Wisely, I decided it was not the time to test his sense of humor. I lugged the smaller suitcases, wondering if we looked as pitiful and comical as I felt hauling all that junk. My fingers kept losing their grip on the handles and eventually I dropped one. Charlie turned around to see if I needed his help as a young man approached from behind and picked it up for me.

"Here," he insisted, "let me carry that for you."

"Thanks." I said grateful for the friendly gesture.

"Americans, yes?"

"Yes. How could you tell?"

He looked meaningfully at all the stuff we were lugging. "A good guess," he snickered. I smiled weakly because of what he meant. His look inferred that only Americans would even own that much stuff and certainly only Americans would be crazy enough to drag it around the world.

With his help Charlie and I boarded the nearest coach and ducked into the first empty compartment to make it our home for the duration of the ride. In spite of the late hour, it was still bright outside since Northern Europe enjoys extremely long hours of daylight during the summer season. We settled down on the soft brown leather seats and I put my sore feet up on one of our bags. I was primed to enjoy the scenery whizzing by our window. The beautiful countryside was blooming with visual delights. How charming were the little eighteenth century cottages, clusters of quaint brick and wooden buildings nestled in protective stands of bushy trees. Then came the endless flat grasslands dotted with flocks of sleeping ducks and herds of somnolent swine.

I planned to ask Charlie if he knew why there were no windmills when the door to our private compartment flew open with a bang. The racket of the rails and the scowl of the conductor standing in the hall startled me. "Tickets," he growled and Charlie handed him our yellow stubs. "You're in the wrong section," he announced struggling to keep his balance. "This is first class. Your tickets are for second class, Car #T that way." He pointed toward the back of the train.

Charlie quickly apologized. "Can we pay the difference and stay in here?"

"No. You have to move." He was adamant after all, he had

his orders too. He backed further down the aisle and waited while we gathered up our stuff.

I fumed and grumbled as we battled our way through two almost empty cars before we reached our assigned seats in Car #T. On the way Charlie reminded me that we were foreigners and the least we could do was to obey the laws of the land. Though our ultimate plans were plain and simple civil disobedience we intended to stay legal for as long as possible.

In less than thirty minutes, the train pulled into Zwolle Station. We tumbled out into the warm evening air just as an astute young taxi driver came running in our direction. After a short discussion about the address of the hotel he started loading our luggage into his cab.

"You're a godsend," I exclaimed when he slammed the lid on the trunk. He didn't understand.

We were ready to leave and Charlie and I plopped ourselves into the back seats and closed our eyes too tired for small talk. It was almost midnight when our taxi stopped in front of an enchanting, three-story chateau sheltered by a stand of poplars. Stars like gemstones glittered in the black sky while a full moon washed the surroundings with silver light. The place reminded me of a storybook setting.

All the luggage was piled on the curb when Charlie paid the fare and the cabby drove away. I couldn't help notice how quiet it was. We picked our way carefully up the stone walk and rang the bell. An outside light came on and a tall, slender, sleepy middle-aged man appeared in the doorway.

"We're with the mission," Charlie explained. "Sorry we're so late."

"Never mind. Come in, come in" he said in a friendly low tone of voice. His welcome immediately put us at ease. "I'll show you to your room."

We followed our host down a dusky hallway and up a long

flight of creaky stairs. He lead us to the last door on the right. Using one of the large keys attached to his belt loop, he turned the handle and the old-fashioned brass lock released with a soft clunk. He moved aside then signaled for us to enter ahead of him. I went in first. A subdued light flowed from a lamp on the nightstand. It cast a welcoming glow over the small, quaintly decorated room.

"Charlie, this is darling," I said, a little too loudly.

"Sh," they responded in concert while bringing in our suitcases.

"Sorry," I whispered.

The innkeeper left, closing the door gently behind him. I set a new record for putting on my pajamas with Charlie not far behind. The taut, clean white sheets and soft feathery pillows had a soothing effect on our tired flesh. As usual, I tucked my Bible under my pillow. Charlie turned out the light and we laid perfectly still though the bed felt like it was shaking. The last sounds I heard were jumbo jet engines roaring overhead and the rhythmic clickity-clack of train wheels very close by.

We knew nothing else until a hammering on the door woke us both out of deep, sound sleep the next morning. I rolled over and groaned as Charlie sat bolt upright. "Who's there?" he called softly.

"John here," our visitor whispered back through the door. "John von Houseman, here to carry you down to the office, eh?"

"Yes, of course," Charlie answered. "We'll be right out. Come on, Chop, we better hurry."

Charlie was half dressed when I dragged myself into the bathroom. I dreaded seeing how much toil would be necessary before I could face the world. The mirror did not lie. My flattened perm made my long hair appear to have a mind of its own. Armed with brush and hair spray I prepared to do battle until Charlie's glare convinced me to make do with an emergency ponytail instead.

John von Houseman, a loving, gentle, charismatic, father figure in his fifties stood in the stairwell watching us descend. He had riveting blue eyes, thick chestnut-colored hair and a short beard. His capacious clothes with multiple pleats made him appear even larger than he actually was. Tall, strong, burgeoning with good health and concealed pockets that was our John.

"Welcome, my friends. Welcome." He extended both hands toward us and we responded happily to his open friendly hugs. He appeared too guileless and vulnerable to be involved in the smuggling business.

"Did we keep you waiting?" Charlie asked.

"Not at all, but we must hurry, eh?"

John kept us moving until I had climbed into the back seat of his black, compact, diesel-fueled Renault. He and Charlie had squeezed into the front bucket seats. As we zipped down a two-lane country road in high gear, he asked the question I wanted most to avoid. "We were afraid you changed your minds and weren't coming, eh. Why were you so late?"

I dismissed it as rhetorical, at least I hoped it was and I was especially pleased when John didn't push for an answer.

On the outskirts of town, he made a right hand turn into the parking lot of a large, plain, cement block warehouse. He pulled to a stop in front of the building that served as mission headquarters.

We unfolded ourselves into the bright warm morning sunshine. Charlie and I breathed deeply and stretched our bodies while John retrieved his briefcase from where I had been sitting in the back seat. It had been well concealed because I never guessed there was anything else beside me.

"Follow me, eh," John said sternly.

He led us inside past a row of offices with closed doors and into a cramped conference room where he invited us to sit down at an oblong table while he squeezed in behind. Strewn across the top were papers, maps and communiqués. John waited watching me patiently as my eyes scanned the sparsely furnished room. Obviously, he never missed anything.

"You leave tomorrow, eh," he said when I finished satisfying my curiosity and faced him again. "But first, we have much material to. . . ." He paused, searching for the proper English word. "How do you say in English, eh . . . ?"

"Review?" I suggested.

"Yes, much material to review. First, let us open with prayer, eh."

"Yes, let's," Charlie and I answered in unison.

John bowed his head and folded his hands to begin a simple conversation with our Heavenly Father. "Lord, we have come together to serve our brothers and sisters, eh. You alone know our hearts and what lies ahead. Speak through us as we commit this day to you."

I prayed next and Charlie closed. We were in agreement. Amen.

John spread out a map of Europe and verbally walked us through our assignment. He had planned a stringent foray into communist territory from beginning to end. We slid to the edges of our chairs, leaning forward to peer at the small red X-marks indicating each target. Several houses and churches, John pinpointed each while tracing the route slowly with his forefinger carefully elaborating on the details of each border crossing — trying to prepare us for any eventuality.

Under the table Charlie's hand reached for mine as we exchanged glances seeking reassurance from each other as our excitement intensified.

We kept working through the lunch hour stopping only

long enough to devour a small sandwich and a piece of plain cake. Somehow the day had slipped away and it was late afternoon before John turned to us and asked, "Questions?"

I immediately recalled Brother Andrew's warning about getting us into countries but not guaranteeing to get us back out. I sighed deeply and shook my head. The only questions I had were ones John could not answer. Jesus alone knew what the future held.

Dinnertime meant that only one item remained on John's list but it was an important one. It was time for him to introduce us to our vehicle and its hidden compartments where his crew had already concealed hundreds of Russian Bibles.

John wrapped up the paperwork part of our orientation and we followed him outside to finish. As usual, I was trotting along trying to keep up when an unexpected wave of nervousness coerced me into a fit of chatter. John flashed me a knowing smile. It was all so exciting, I could hardly wait to get started.

Then we saw it.

Unfortunately, there was no way to prepare us for the initial shock. This was it, our assigned temporary home-on-wheels. Charlie and I gaped. Our mouths were locked open, our eyes bulged. We could hardly focus on the monstrosity, a baby blue, aluminum, cab-over camper mounted on a white one ton Ford truck brandishing Florida license plates. The shell extended out at least two feet on both sides and from the rear end of the flat bed. It was a circus car, a pony cart hauling a gigantic elephant. Stunned by its preposterous measurements and ungainly appearance, I could not move.

"What's wrong?" John asked innocently.

"Wrong?" I finally unfroze and circled around back to see if it really was as enormous as it first appeared. It was. "Ha, don't try to kid me John, I know what you're up to," I said. "This is one of those jokes where the kids first tell their parents something really horrible because the awful truth is not nearly as bad and they want to prepare . . . ."

John looked puzzled and I knew he didn't have a clue what I was talking about.

"You mean, you're not kidding," I said with some hesitation, "it's really not a joke, is it?"

John chuckled and shook his head. "No, it's not a joke. It's really not bad at all, eh. Come on, take a closer look."

I glanced at Charlie, who looked like I felt. Our blissful excitement had dissolved into clouds of disbelief and misgivings. Granted, God's ways are not our ways, but surely, this bordered on lunacy.

"John," I said, with apparently superior wisdom, "tell me that nobody is going to suspect we're not up to something."

"Don't worry, this vehicle has made many, many successful trips, eh," John replied then hastened to encourage us with a recital of the outstanding career of the baby blue behemoth. I wasn't convinced. We would surely be asking for trouble by drawing unnecessary attention to ourselves.

Something else also bothered me. I planned to do most of the driving because the maps were difficult to decipher and my vision was extremely poor on detail. Charlie would do what he did best, navigate. In my worst nightmare, I had never been behind the wheel of such an unwieldy giant. The prospect took my breath away.

"What else is available?" I stammered.

"This is it," John answered firmly. Baby Blue was already pregnant with precious cargo and there was no alternative. "Perhaps, you want to try her out, eh?" he asked wearing his usual gentle smile.

"No, thanks. Tomorrow will be soon enough," I responded hoping the delay would give me time to summon up my courage.

By the time Charlie and I dragged ourselves back to the hotel it was early evening. As far as we were concerned the day was almost over.

My husband was ravenous so we headed toward the inn's quaint dining room, decorated in Dutch blue and white. Only two other couples were being served when we arrived and we hoped that was not a statement about the quality of the food. I settled for a small salad but Charlie, who takes his food seriously, ordered the special: appetizer, soup, bread, cheese, entree and a good old American banana split. Everything was delicious.

Our tummies were satisfied and our bodies were tired so we went to bed. At 9:30, we both lay there staring at the ceiling. Was it true that tomorrow we would begin a long journey in John's outlandish vehicle through lovely, free Holland; through industrious, free West Germany; through tightly-guarded, communist Czechoslovakia, where the penalty for smuggling Bibles was a mandatory year in prison; and then deep into rebellious, communist Poland to within ninety miles of the Soviet border?

What if Murphy's Law is true, that if something can go wrong it will? What if that big, fat baby blue thing breaks down? What if we get caught? What if a civil war breaks out? What if I get separated from Charlie? What if my yellow streak gets wider than it already is and completely wraps itself around my body?

I rolled over. "Honey, are you still awake?"

"Uh huh. I can't sleep."

"Me, neither. Charlie, I'm scared. If the authorities find the Bibles what will they do to us? If they put us in prison will anybody know? Will anybody come get us out? You don't suppose Jesus would let them put us in jail, do you?"

"I don't know. What do you want to do? Should we forget it? Just go on home, sing in the choir and go to Sunday

School? Vacation in Honolulu? Take a Caribbean cruise like normal people?"

I leaned up on my elbow, surprised at his words. "Charles, are you being facetious or are you serious? Remember what Pastor said?"

"What? Refresh my memory." He turned toward me, gave me a hug and a kiss on the cheek.

"You know," I said, "his statement about missing out on a blessing by ignoring God's call. I think his exact words were, 'Don't shoot yourself in the foot or you'll slow down your walk as a Christian.' You were kidding about going home, weren't you?"

"I think I was, I hope so. But it's impossible for me to comprehend communism, to even imagine what it's like to live in submission to a ruthless government. A country where the bureaucrats are determined to control by force, if necessary, every aspect of your life. Where leaders refuse to become accountable to any reasonable, definable justice system and have no absolute moral standards of their own. Tell me, how did it happen? The civilized world used to have a semblance of biblical standards. Americans were at least respected in Europe. If we got into trouble with the foreign authorities our embassies would bail us out. But now? I don't know, Chop. I don't want to back out but I'm not sure what to expect. At least at home you can pretty much count on what will happen tomorrow." So the struggle raged inside of him as well.

"Charlie, pray with me, okay?" I asked nervously.

We knelt together alongside the bed and waited quietly on the Holy Spirit to move on our faltering humanity. Charlie prayed with thanksgiving for God's faithfulness in bringing us safely this far.

Then he said, "Please Lord, You promised in Your Word to go before us and make the crooked ways straight. That's what we need tomorrow and the next day, Lord, and we thank You for it."

The anxiety in his voice touched me. He sounded changed from the always self-confident, irrepressible Charlie. Now he sounded vulnerable, something I had not discerned in him before.

We crawled back under the covers. He slipped his arm over my shoulder and pulled me gently toward himself. I cuddled closer to his side. His physical strength was comforting since I realized that I was physically unequal to the task. I had come to the place where Jesus' strength and my weakness met. I took heart because He said: Without me ye can do nothing . . . but My strength is made perfect in weakness.

Weak, we were. More than ever we realized how much we needed Him if we were even going to survive.

3
Czechoslovakian Crossing

The next morning, Charlie read to me from the book of Hebrews: "Remember them that are in bonds, as bound with them; and them which suffer adversity, as being yourselves also in the body . . . for he hath said, I will never leave thee, nor forsake thee. So that we may boldly say, The Lord is my helper, and I will not fear what man shall do unto me."

He had just finished the verse when we heard the distinctive rattling noise of John's diesel coming through the open window. There was no mistaking the sound, we recognized it immediately. Perfect timing. We were ready to go and could not have planned it better had we tried.

Charlie closed the book and I grabbed my purse. We hurried downstairs heading for the front door when Charlie stopped to make sure he had the room keys.

While he was searching though his pockets I went outside. I stood on the porch and thought I caught the hint of lilacs in the air. I paused for a second, closed my eyes and took a long deep breath. The fragrance was delightful. Amazing how God's word had renewed my faltering courage — I felt alive with hope and expectation. *How grateful I am for the energy the good Lord sends into every new day,* I thought to myself.

Charlie ended my reverie when he reached for my hand as he walked by — we had work to do. John was standing beside the car reading over his notes when we approached him.

"Good morning, good morning," he said with the guttural Dutch accent we sometimes tried to imitate.

We returned his greeting and John handed Charlie what appeared to be a shopping list. Without wasting any more time we all climbed into the car feeling very comfortable with each other.

After a few minutes of cordial chitchat John suggested we stop by the local grocery store to purchase the supplies we needed for our trip. Charlie and I agreed after I made sure I had our traveler's checks with me. The small family market was opening just as we arrived.

We shopped the aisles under John's careful supervision. He warned us about Eastern Europe's pitifully poor sanitary conditions and significant shortages. There were major necessities to stock up on, especially toilet tissue, and we reached the checkout counter with a cart full of items.

Loading the bags, boxes and ourselves into John's small car became a comedy of errors. It took three different attempts before we finally fit everything in. Fortunately, we didn't have very far to go.

My legs were beginning to ache from straddling the hump in the floor so when the car stopped beside the camper I made a quick exit. I glanced over at the truck, the one we had nicknamed Baby Blue wondering what the inside was like. I decided I couldn't wait to see and hurried on ahead leaving Charlie and John to deal with the groceries.

Acting as though I knew what I was doing, I opened the back door, hurdled the high step into the living area and felt my way through the darkness. A sliver of light helped me locate the thick curtains intended to keep inquisitive people from looking in. Daylight poured through the window when I brushed them aside and I spun around not really knowing what to expect.

To my great relief, the inside turned out to be a pleasant surprise. Blended earth tones made the living room warm and glowing. The gold and green striped fabrics even complemented the oak veneer cabinets. A creme-colored naugahyde bench wrapped itself around three sides of the kitchen table across from a stainless steel sink. Only the bright orange counter tops looked out of place and clashed with the matching avocado stove and refrigerator.

There was only one problem with our house on wheels, the bed. It was small. The mattress extended out over the cab and two people of medium build could probably manage but poor Charlie. His legs were too long for him to get comfortable. Obviously, my husband was in for some sleepless nights. Nevertheless, this was home for awhile so we would learn to live with it.

By the time, I finished unpacking our supplies, the cabinets bulged and the refrigerator door barely closed. Charlie was a hearty eater, even for a husky man, still I doubted we would ever finish eating all that food by ourselves.

We had given John most of our religious reading material including my precious Bible the day before. However, he let us keep a few cassette tapes of Christian music because the titles did not identify the contents for what they really were. It was far too dangerous for us to carry anything else alluding to our Christian faith across the border. Now it was time for Charlie and I to complete the process John started.

According to John's instructions, we had to memorize all the details of the hand drawn maps and personal notes including all the names and phone numbers we received. Afterward, when we felt confident about remembering everything we were to destroy them. There must not be any evidence linking us to the mission or any other contacts behind the Curtain.

Finally, John gave us a last minute review and reminded us to fill our fifty-five gallon gas tank. We had no further questions.

Now everything was ready — it was time to go.

Saying good-bye was especially difficult. John's unexpected tenderness toward us had been a real comfort during our two hectic days of training. Under his care, we had thrived on sweet Christian fellowship so when our hands grasped for the last time, Charlie and I both were fighting tears.

At 2:00 p.m., I climbed into the driver's seat to take control of Baby Blue. I squared my shoulders, breathed deeply and turned the ignition key. The engine's roar helped to shake off the sad sentimental feelings by reminding me of why we had come. Cautiously, I shifted into low gear and we started down the long, bumpy, unpaved driveway.

We reached the intersection and I came to a rolling stop before starting to turn onto the main highway. The road was empty so I stepped on the gas pedal then jammed on the brakes when Charlie yelled, "Stop! We're going to hit the fence."

The truck jerked to a standstill sending cargo flying into all new positions and my stomach up into my throat.

"Chop, please be careful! No one is going to be very happy with us if we wreck their camper you know," Charlie sounded as nervous as I was.

"I know, I'm sorry, I didn't see it," I said defensively. "I have a feeling this rig will be the death of me. Are you sure I'm supposed to drive?"

"No, I'm not. But would you rather risk getting lost or not getting there at all? It's up to you."

He had a point. "Never mind, I'll drive," I said and gritted my teeth.

Charlie leaned out the window and guided me forward ever so slowly. Baby Blue's overhanging shell barely cleared the wooden post marking the corner of the property. My husband raised his eyebrows in amazement and I wondered what he was thinking. Maybe, I was better off not knowing.

John followed us on foot and waved us off when he saw we were safely on our way. Would we would ever see him again?

At last we were rolling and I relaxed. So far, so good.

I pulled into a petrol station on the outskirts of town and it took an entire fifty-five gallons to fill the tank. Charlie began chatting with Hans, the attendant, who was curious about Americans while the pump was running. Meanwhile, I strolled around back to check the door latch. All was well, I thought, until I noticed the sidewall on the rear tire appeared to be separating. I mentioned it to Charlie as he paid Hans with a handful of guilders.

He decided to check it out and crouched down to see the split from eye level. "You're right Chop, I can't believe it but we already have vehicle problems."

Our eyes met and I read his mind. I felt sure we both had the same thought: *Is nothing on this trip ever going to be easy?*

"Well," he said rubbing his chin, "if I use the spare now and we get a flat later we'll really have a serious problem on our hands. Maybe, I can buy a tire from Hans."

Predictably, Hans did not have a tire to fit. There was nothing else to do: We had to call John.

Charlie went inside to try to reach him while I stood guard and prayed. He soon emerged with a smile on his face and informed me that John kept a spare at the gas station across from the market only a few blocks away.

Dilemma solved by 5 p.m., we were on the road again. This time it was Charlie's turn to drive. He was cruising with the windows down listening to an English radio station when we agreed we needed a coffee break.

I wriggled through the modified opening of the shell to reach the kitchen and perked a pot of Dutch coffee on one of the gas burners. How neat to perform my first domestic chore on the trip so far. The strong hot brew laced with caffeine tasted delicious and gave us our second wind.

We were beginning to feel better about everything. Since crossing little Holland would be a snap we could reach West Germany and spend our first night in a nice, clean rest stop on the Autobahn. At least that was the plan until the cars in front of us slowed to a crawl. Sadly, we were caught in the makings of a horrendous traffic jam and burned up the next three hours in stop-and-go traffic.

It was almost dark when Charlie pulled over and we switched drivers at the West German border. I settled in behind the wheel just as a light rain began falling. I flicked on the wipers and they swept the windshield clear except for the water that impaired my line of vision — a universal phenomenon.

The radio station had signed off the air and before I knew it, Charlie fell asleep.

I was holding my speed at 45 mph when the lush level landscape turned hilly and we started up a long grade. The cars in front of us all seemed to be losing momentum and I was worried whether Baby Blue could climb the steep incline. I wanted to avoid getting stuck behind the slow moving car pulling a trailer in front of me. A glance into the rearview mirror showed I had enough clearance to pass and I was growing impatient. Without giving it a second thought I mashed the accelerator down to the floor to shift into passing gear and pulled out.

As the speedometer climbed I rose up slightly on the edge of my seat to adjust my grip on the steering wheel. Suddenly, a huge semitrailer pulled in behind me seemingly from out of nowhere. Practically riding my bumper, he kept flashing his headlights for me to move out of his way. His hovering presence made me extremely nervous but I was unable to change lanes again because of the solid line of traffic to my right. At that point, the road narrowed and a flimsy yellow guardrail was all that separated me from the oncoming traffic with their blinding headlights.

The vacuum from a huge speeding truck passing in the opposite direction created a draft. It yanked the steering wheel almost completely out of my hands. I momentarily lost control and veered to the left dangerously close to the rail. My reflexes reacted within a split second and I straightened the wheels.

Meanwhile, the pavement kept flying by. By then I was going over 60 mph. I squinted into the right side view mirror and saw that the long procession of traffic stayed packed tightly together. What could I do? I was stuck in the passing lane.

If that wasn't bad enough, at that moment, the sky unzipped, exploding like a wall of water. It blinded me temporarily and I quickly reached for the wiper switch to turn it up to high. It was of little help; I could hardly see.

My palms poured sweat and I feared I would die of heart failure. In desperation, I cried out to God praying the same prayer over and over: *Our Father, Who art in heaven. Our Father, Who art in heaven. My Father, Who art in heaven. Help me, help us.*

I squinted into the distance and saw our exit sign rapidly approaching. Somehow, I had to maneuver into the right lane and quickly. I checked the mirror again but the cars were still coming in what appeared to be a solid line. Maybe I could force an opening? Maybe my guardian angel . . . .

My mind was in turmoil: What would I do if I missed the exit? With a quick decision, I signaled my intentions to change lanes and started edging over. Evidently, I was cutting off the car behind me because the driver blared his horn as I swerved sharply to the right and escaped onto the ramp into the darkness.

Startled by the sound, Charlie woke up from his nap and looked over at me. "Huh? What happened? What was that?" he asked still sounding groggy.

"Oh, nothing," I answered feebly.

We had made it as far as Nuremberg and I parked our camper under the shelter of the gas station's metal canopy. Fortunately, by now the rain had slowed to drizzle. I still felt weak from the aftermath of our near mishap and decided to wait in the cab while Charlie topped off the tank. He climbed back into the passenger's seat and was busy counting Deutsche marks when I turned the key to start the engine. Nothing happened.

"It might be damp. Wait a minute then try again," he said.

I waited then turned the key again. And again. And again. Nothing.

"What do we do now?" I asked my weary husband.

Charlie sighed and slipped his husky hand around mine. He sounded tired as he prayed to our Father for help. Apparently, Father heard because when I turned the key again the engine responded with a roar. We were grateful but enough was enough. I pulled over to the edge of the parking lot, turned off the ignition and we called it a day.

The next morning, after an early breakfast at the rest stop cafeteria, we returned to our home-on-wheels. I sat in the driver's seat and turned the ignition key — nothing happened. In response, I leaned over the steering wheel, dropped my head and Charlie groaned. How frustrating, more trouble and it wasn't even nine o'clock.

Charlie climbed out, opened the hood and after poking around for a few minutes located the difficulty. A wiring harness had shaken loose, dangling two inches from its connection. Two inches? It had been an absolute miracle that we had been able to drive the night before. After all, we had moved quite a distance from under the shelter to the edge of the lot, a specific answer to Charlie's prayer. I was ready to write it down, but first Charlie needed a short piece of wire to fix the problem so I began an intensive scavenger hunt in the kitchen.

I asked the Lord to give me eyes to see. The search continued. I was almost ready to quit until I opened the refrigerator door. Now the answer to our problem was in plain view. Our solution was presently holding the end of a cellophane wrapper on a loaf of bread closed — a metal tie. I unfastened it and hurried outside to show Charlie. Charlie looked doubtful when he noticed me waving my prize in the air.

He scraped the plastic from the twisted wire with his pocket knife and studied it for a moment. "Here goes," he muttered.

He disappeared under the hood and within minutes had it fastened securely in place.   Now the question was would it work?

Since there was only one way to find out I jumped into the driver's seat, held my breath and turned the key. A miracle. The engine instantly kicked over with a ferocious roar. Supernaturally, the old Ford motor purred for the next twenty-two hundred miles while our faithful Father God — or one of His angels — held the two ends of Charlie's improvised repair together.

At midday, Charlie was driving when we approached the Czechoslovakian border. There was no way to miss the "Off Limits" signs warning military personnel about the border inasmuch as they lined the highway. They made me nervous because beyond lay the most difficult juncture in Eastern Europe. It carried the highest penalty — one full year imprisonment — if the authorities discovered the Bibles. We could feel the demonic pressure intensifying. Should the material be discovered we were on our own since we had our orders not to put anyone else in jeopardy.

We were within striking distance when Charlie pulled off into the last rest area about one quarter mile before the crossing.

It was time to burn any newly accumulated documentation in the kitchen sink. I began tearing the list of names, addresses, locations, phone numbers, and instructions into small pieces. Meanwhile, Charlie located a pack of matches and plunged the burning tip into the mound of scraps. It took a moment to ignite then suddenly a yellow flame leapt into the air. We stepped back quickly watching until it petered out. The residue, however, continued to smolder until the room was filled with smoke. Charlie and I started to choke.

"Great move, Mr. Bond," I said, trying unsuccessfully to make a joke.

Charlie ignored me and I knew why.

As newcomers to the world of espionage and intrigue we didn't know whether to laugh or not. We fanned the smoke, rubbed our eyes and cleaned up the ashes then pulled back into the line of traffic. That's when it really dawned on me: This was no spy novel. This was no TV program. This was real life. What we were about to do was dangerous to both life and limb. Within the hour we could be on our way to jail.

My moment of reckoning had come. Charlie had already made his peace but the depth of my personal commitment to this ministry was again under serious scrutiny: *Am I prepared to give up my life for my friends? How about people I don't even know?*

Evidently, God had not stopped to consider whether I meant it when I conceded to His will and said, "Here am I; send me." He just heard what I said and He answered, "All right, I'll send you. Go!"

I studied Charlie to try to discern what he might be thinking. Our relationship had already weathered some difficult situations at home. In spite of the trials, we had a lumpy, good, solid marriage. Now I wondered if he had any regrets. He wasn't volunteering any information so I didn't ask.

We drove another few miles, traffic began slowing and in

the distance we could see the border. I noticed a small white car parked on the other side of the road about twenty feet from the gate. Next to it a middle-aged man, two children and probably the man's wife huddled together watching the ruthless legal and public rape of their belongings.

Were the border guards state employees or bandits? I wondered and watched. With gang-like tactics they yanked out the back seat and propped it up against the three suitcases lying open on the ground. One guard scrutinized the engine compartment while another rifled though their personal possessions. Such blatant tyranny, stripping men of their dignity, their rights as human beings and insulting their similitude to God, bore a grim illustration of man's universal inhumanity to man.

I was transfixed by the sight when Charlie called my attention back to the road. He pointed to the tall, thin gawky guard standing next to the car in front of us.

"Why, he's only a boy," I whispered.

I'm not sure what kind of villains I had expected but the boy was only a kid with a rifle. His khaki uniform hung on his underdeveloped frame and his trousers draped down to his shoes. The semiautomatic slung over his left shoulder, however, kept any compassion we might feel in perspective. He was, after all, a trained killer with the authority to shoot people when necessary.

I remembered that Czechoslovakia was very much a police state where Big Brother did not promote civil rights. Then my enemy mentality faded until I no longer saw that side of him. He was simply a soul needing to know the Savior. *Love the sinner, hate the sin,* I chided myself. I wondered how he would react to the gospel under different circumstances and I sent up a prayer that the right Christian witness would come into his life someday.

The car in front of us pulled away and we glided into first

place directly across from the boy. Suddenly, we were face-to-face and I noticed the light hairs on his chin were so thin that I doubted he even shaved. I smiled when I handed him our documents and watched closely as he sifted through them.

"American. American." I cried jovially. He showed no outward response or any interest in our papers. He handed them back and kept silent. Without making eye contact with me at all, he turned sideways and signaled for us to move on.

We went another twenty feet where we stopped to wait again but this encounter would not be so casual. The guard appeared to be pure Slav. He had thick unruly hair and a heavy mustache that barely concealed an old and ugly scar across the middle of his upper lip and nose. He approached the cab on the passenger side and stood in front of Charlie. "Papers!" he demanded, stiff and square. His demeaning tone sent shivers up my spine. The red stars pinned to his lapel signified a superior rank and I braced for trouble.

Charlie held our documents out the window and the guard snatched them from his hand without saying another word. We were at his mercy. He knew it and he wanted us to know it — all part of the evil process designed to intimidate. It worked very well.

He examined each item separately then stared at us. His dark eyes probed deeply as if he knew I was concealing something. Against my will, I broke eye contact and only occasionally glanced in his direction. He said something in Czech to Charlie and his loud raspy voice startled me. His mouth turned upward in a sneer as if he enjoyed badgering. He held my passport in his hand and leaned around Charlie eyeing me up and down like a lecher then paused to compare my face with the picture. He yanked his head back, cocked it to one side, laughed and looked down his nose at us while stroking his thick neck. It was quite a show and we were, to make a bad joke, a captive audience. He made a clucking sound, turned and walked back toward the patrol shack leaving us sitting there alone.

Fear, like I had never experienced before swept over me. Almost in tears, I reached for Charlie's hand. "What's going on?" I whispered. "It's like these hoodlums were expecting us and now that we're here they're trying to decide who will take us in."

"Take it easy, Chop. Don't let your imagination run away with you. Nothing has happened yet; maybe he's suffering with a toothache and his dentist is in Switzerland. Who knows? Just act natural, like we're waiting for lunch to be served."

Charlie's halfhearted joke about the guard having a dentist in Switzerland made me giggle inside and I felt a little better. But time dragged — ten minutes, twenty. Then suddenly I remembered, "Never will I leave you; never will I forsake you." So that we may boldly say, "The Lord is my helper; I will not fear what man shall do unto me." I will not fear.

We waited quietly, neither Charlie nor I heard him return until his raucous voice jolted us both when he shouted, "Get out!"

Immediately, we left the cab and he climbed into the front seat. He bounced his large body vigorously up and down on the cushions. All the while I was hoping a spring would pop loose. What was he trying to locate, buried treasure? The thought amused me. A pun of sorts: earthly treasure versus God's treasure. Then the reality of the moment drained all the humor out of it. Of course, he found nothing but he wasn't through with us yet. Not yet. Now he signaled for Charlie to open the back of the camper and they climbed inside closing the door behind them.

I turned around wondering if anyone was watching me. If they were what should I do? Body language is revealing so I decided to stroll around the camper trying to act nonchalant to avoid delivering any message that might be misconstrued as anything other than peaceful boredom. At the same time, my inner turmoil was indescribable. My heart pounded in concert with my silent cries unto God for deliverance. I cast my faith in with the Hebrew children recalling their ordeal in the fiery furnace and God's faithfulness on their behalf. God could rescue us, but would He?

Intently, I tried to hear what was happening on the inside between Charlie and the guard who was rummaging through the camper determined to find contraband. But all his wretched banging, slamming, kicking, pressing, pushing on the interior proved nothing. He found nothing! Zero! Zilch! The God who makes blind eyes see, sometimes makes seeing eyes blind.

After what seemed like an eternity Charlie and the snoop reappeared. The guard's red face said it all. I knew that he knew. He snarled in frustration as he handed over our papers and motioned for us to move on to the booth where we would exchange some of our travelers' checks for korunas and buy gas coupons.

For us, the hardest part was over but the ordeal was not. After all, that was only the first gate. Ahead were still several miles of empty road through a thick, booby-trapped forest laced with land mines known as no-man's land. For anyone fleeing the communist state the deadly forest stood waiting.

I gazed out the open window remembering the Old Testament promise, "I will even make a way in the wilderness." God, please make it true for us.

The second gate loomed in the distance so I slowed ready to stop until the guard raised the red and white bar and waved us through. What an eerie feeling knowing that we were leaving our freedoms behind to enter the world where communism was god.

A few miles later, I turned into a rest stop where Charlie

went one way while I went the other to locate the facilities. Then we remembered John's warning about the bathroom dilemma—there were none. With no alternative, I returned to the truck, grabbed a roll of toilet tissue, gritted my teeth and headed for the bushes. *How tacky,* I told myself, *but you better get used to it. This is going to be a long trip.*

The occupants of the only other car parked there ignored me as I passed by them. We were all in the same predicament. Still, I could feel my face turn beet red. "There's no place like home," I commented to Charlie afterward. He only laughed as he drove away. Men had it easy on a picnic.

With each monotonous mile we delved deeper into Satan's domain as our own spiritual battles continued. We could expect our struggle with the world, the flesh and the devil to intensify in the days to come as we began to understand the spirit of our mission a little better. For us to penetrate the forces of evil and gain ground for the Master would take dogged determination. We needed ears to hear what the Spirit was saying to us. Dark depression hung over the entire area like a thick fog. The spiritual blackness was real, almost palpable.

I realized with a shudder, that this is what eventually develops when a government or powerful group of rebels violently—or even slowly but inexorably—usurps the freedoms, the lives and the very souls of the people. First, religion is ridiculed as "the opium of the people." Adherents of Christianity are particularly ridiculed then harassed. Then, certain literature—the Bible, for example—is outlawed at school, then in public and finally at home. Laws are passed. Free speech including prayer is suppressed and history textbooks are "corrected" and rewritten. The press becomes a tool of government; media events replace truth. More new laws require imprisonment or execution for political troublemakers and literary lawbreakers. Finally, the shedding of innocent blood becomes commonplace.

Time passed and we continued our trek.

The landscape at first impressed us as being charming almost quaint until we looked more closely at the poverty and the faces of the people. We saw so many poor farmers and villages, one after another. And every farm had its quota of Eastern European bag ladies, pathetic old women in communist countries who till the ground until they fall dead. My heart went out to them. They reminded me of my grandmother who immigrated from Slovakia to America many years ago. My roots are in this part of the world. How I thanked my heavenly Father for that brave woman once again because she made it possible for me to be born in America. Always, it seems, when anyone from any place in the world wants to leave their roots to start over in a new place, where do they want to go? To America, the land of the free. Oh, that it might always be so!

Horse drawn wagons driven by sad faced, gray bearded men with faithful dogs at their sides occasionally dominated the road. They seemed locked in a time warp — like riding a time capsule back to the Eighteenth Century. I noticed all the communities had one common, modern denominator, the disgraceful stigma of a failed church. Some buildings were boarded up and overgrown with weeds, others converted into factories or motels.

"Look, Charlie," I said, pointing to an old church set back off the highway. Trash was piled as high as the tall, iron fence surrounding the decrepit structure while boards covered all the windows and a padlock hung from the front door. The appalling sight made me ponder the circumstances that would cause such grievous abandonment of a once lovely and lively place of fellowship. Only the crumbling brick and mortar remained to suggest the answer. It stood lifeless and defamed as incriminating evidence perpetually testifying against the apathy of an unaware, uncaring Christendom. Bleak catacombs draped with spider webs and blanketed with dust had replaced the lofty cathedrals where the faithful once gathered, a tragic reflection of heathen power over a once vigorous and prosperous, now powerless, people.

Surely, this could never happen in America!

Our progress was slow. Narrow roads reduced our average speed to 35 mph while gas restrictions on each tank forced us to make frequent stops at filling stations. Ten liters per coupon was all we were allowed. The thrill of our initial victory at the border crossing subsided during the next eleven hundred dreary miles between our entry and our destination. We had two days of hard travel ahead of us.

By dusk, according to Charlie's calculations we were only about twenty miles from Prague, the legendary city that once hosted kings and queens, renowned artisans and scores of intelligentsia. We hoped to arrive in time to see some sights but darkness was already snatching at the meager bit of remaining daylight.

We followed the illuminated signs indicating the center of town and as we approached I peered into the distance. "Charlie, talk about déjè vu, this place looks vaguely familiar. I think I've seen it before."

Also confused by the familiarity of our surroundings, Charlie turned on the interior light and held up the map for a bearing on our location. As nearly as he could tell we had made one big circle back to where we had been an hour before.

Bleary-eyed, I pulled the truck over and stopped under a cement overpass. My shoulders drooped under what felt like a hundred pounds of fatigue. I leaned my forehead against the wheel while rubbing the back of my neck. Charlie studied the map without success. We were lost, engulfed in darkness and there was nothing to do but wait for morning.

We climbed back into the shell where I collapsed on the bed while Charlie rustled up something to eat.

Propped on one elbow, I voiced my perspective on what our tomorrow might bring. "We have twenty-four hours to do one of two things: either cross Czechoslovakia or locate a police station to have our visas signed. Our going in circles trying to follow that map places our curfew in serious jeopardy. Yet a visit to the local constable for his blessing is out of the question, right? The gas gauge registers one-quarter tank and we have no idea when a station may appear. Should we turn around and go back or continue onward? We could very well wind up stranded thousands of miles from home and, of course, unable to speak the language. If we are caught it might mean jail. Otherwise, everything is great and we're right on schedule." Charlie had a faraway look in his eyes. "Charlie," I said "were you listening?"

"Come on, Chop, let's eat."

"Charles!" My voice rose at least two octaves. "How can you think of food at a time like this."

Charlie simply grinned at me. "What else can we do? Worrying won't change anything so we might as well eat. What can I fix you?"

I shook my head in amazement, laughed and fell backwards on the bed. "You're hopeless," I said and pulled the top sheet up over my head. The crunchy sound of Charlie's chomping on his pre-dinner chocolate chip cookie lulled me into a dreamless sleep and he had to eat alone.

Early morning sunlight peering through our windows began to heat the camper like an oven. *Where were we?* Our four feet hit the floor almost simultaneously with a resounding thud as we dragged ourselves into the new day.

Charlie spread the map out over the hood as we pondered our every alternative. Then a Czech car, the infamous Skoda, pulled over to an abrupt stop next to us. The driver, a young man in overalls and a cap, stepped out and greeted us with a verbal spray of the national vernacular.

Using sign language, Charlie and I earnestly tried explaining our dilemma. We quickly realized that though our new acquaintance understood not a word of English he was there to help us.

Charlie pointed to Prague on the map and the man became terribly excited. His voice rose as he waved his arms and chattered away in his native tongue. We watched him, dumbfounded.

I said to Charlie, "Why is he so excited? What do you suppose he's trying to tell us?"

"I don't have a clue," he answered.

The man stepped back into his car, pointed to the road over the underpass and motioned for us to follow him. We shrugged our shoulders with some reservation, climbed into Baby Blue and tailed him for a short distance until he waved us off to the right. Suddenly, the Czechoslovakian countryside was transformed into a bustling metropolis and the welcome sight of a petrol station appeared on the horizon.

Within minutes, we reached downtown Prague during rush hour and traffic was a nightmare. Our teeth rattled as we drove the cobblestone streets watching for signs to Warsaza. We were determined to keep our curfew and reach Poland by the next day. With our first hurdle solidly behind us we felt a renewed divine enthusiasm about what Jesus might do with us next. We were slowly becoming accustomed to living in the miraculous and holding tight to the unseen hand.

4
The Drop

It was early afternoon when we approached the Polish border. As usual, cars from both directions lined up at the crossing barriers. We waited behind a Mercedes coupe with German license plates.

After a forty-minute delay, we crept slowly toward the guards and the gates. I discerned a radical change in the atmosphere different than the consuming oppression of Czechoslovakia. A laissez-faire attitude existed among the officers. We hoped their complacent mood meant the process would be quick and simple because we were eager to pursue our journey. We wanted to see this part of God's world from a Polish perspective, his excellent creation but especially the precious people for whom Jesus died.

Finally, it was our turn and Charlie pulled to a stop at the inspection station. We stood beside the truck as a young, plump guard approached. He wore his green, hard, military hat cocked back off his forehead, and the beginnings of a smile or smirk, I wasn't sure which.

The guard stopped beside Charlie but instead of collecting our papers he unexpectedly whirled around and shouted angrily at one of his comrades who was crossing the median. His more or less carefree expression completely changed and he began frantically waving his arms while the other man continued to ignore him. The spittle collecting at the sides of his mouth sprayed both the air and my husband. I thought I smelled alcohol.

We watched his performance through wide eyes, with mouths open and hearts thumping, hoping his sudden anger would not be turned against us. The tension mounted. A chill of fear raced up and down my spine. He faced us, but only for a moment. Then it seemed as though he had second thoughts because he turned back and began shouting again. Apparently, whatever he said finally triggered a response and the other guard started screaming as they drew closer together. It sounded to us as if they were cursing each other.

"Why did we have to get the only lunatic in the entire place?" I murmured to Charlie, who did not answer me. When the almost unbelievable scene turned into a bout of pushing and shoving, I really became frightened. What a nightmare! My eyes raced back and forth hoping that someone, anyone might notice and intervene. No one did; instead, they simply ignored them.

The two guards went at it hot and heavy, and we had to jump out of the way of their flailing fists. Being helpless to do much physically I prayed for them to stop before one of them was seriously hurt. Minutes later, I was extremely grateful when the fistfight waned into a glaring nose-to-nose confrontation as each man stepped away cautiously. The test of wills ended. Once more it was just three of us and the guard was again smiling at us and sucking his lips. I could hardly believe it. I stared at him, this guard who could transform himself instantly from an infuriated version of Mohammed Ali into a Rodney Dangerfield seeking a little respect.

He beamed while scanning through our documents. At that point, I was sure one of us was crazy. "Disneyland!" he exclaimed with glee. I dismissed the entire episode as some cultural misunderstanding and returned his smile. Charlie simply nodded. Poland was in the midst of radical political change, but if this fellow was an example of the system, the war was over.

Suddenly, the guard disappeared into his little brick hut.

"Why do they always do that?" I asked Charlie.

"Do what?"

"Their disappearing act."

Charlie laughed. "How do you know what they always do, Chop? This is only our second border crossing, you know."

I rolled my eyes at him playfully. "I know, but for some reason I feel like we've done this a million times already."

We quickly ran out of conversation, knowing there were still risks ahead. Neither Charlie nor I wanted to establish our reputation either at home or with John as the smugglers who lost the truck to the authorities. Owning a Bible in Poland was not illegal; what was illegal was transporting Russian Bibles across the border without declaring them to customs. If they discovered our concealed literature, Baby Blue would be confiscated, the Bibles sold on the black market, and we would be detained until we paid a fine, a steep one probably in American dollars. Admittedly, we had a little cash but not enough to buy our way out of jail.

According to John, bribery had become the solution to almost any infringement and corruption the road to survival for many destitute economies in Europe. Granted, we came willing to make whatever sacrifice it would take to accomplish our delivery, even so we never ceased looking to God for our protection and seeking His approval.

Soon our unpredictable guard returned. Without further ado he waved us on our way. Charlie and I both let out a deep sigh of relief.

Charlie took the wheel and followed the narrow road that curved to the left into the gently rolling countryside. The landscape continued as before, a panorama of dying farms, dilapidated villages and ramshackle houses with one added dimension, incredibly nasty pollution. An enormous power plant loomed on the horizon, its four large chimneys spewing an ominous, steady stream of dark smoke into the daytime sky.

We quickly rolled up the windows to keep the stench from floating inside the cab, but we weren't quick enough. The toxic odor was enough to make me gag and Charlie's eyes sting. The worst smog in Los Angeles was nothing compared to this.

We had been driving for several miles when my stomach growled long and deep, announcing lunch time. I hated the idea of stopping and wasting time on our tight schedule even more than I hated to cook. So Charlie and I settled for a couple of oat-raisin granola bars.

Oats. There was just something about eating oats that left me feeling woozy, maybe a hangover from my younger days involved with show horses. Had our granola bars not been glued together with honey and brown sugar I might have passed. But when I remembered John's description of the horrors of living with dire shortages of food, gasoline, heating oil and nearly every other commodity caused by all the black-market confusion, I was humbled and shamed. Shortages of all kinds had hit Poland hard. Her economic system was out of control, fringing on chaos, keeping the people in a chronic state of uncertainty. Only high government officials had plenty of everything, and they weren't sharing. In honor of John's wise counsel, I decided I liked oats, and was thankful for the granola bars.

Two hours passed without incident and we were alone on the highway when I commented to Charlie about how much brighter the future was beginning to appear. He agreed with me, until ironically at that precise moment, we encountered our first political demonstration. Charlie slowed as we approached a crowd of old men, young boys, stocky women, beautiful girls and little children marching behind a Catholic priest. A huge crucifix with a golden image of Christ's broken body loomed high above their heads. It glistened in the bright sunlight. *How exciting*, I thought as we passed by. It was a statement by the Polish Church who had waved her belligerent fist in the face of the communistic evil for decades. Not even the government had been able to overcome the will of the Catholic Poles. The State may have owned their bodies, but never their souls.

We were watching history in the making, and I scooted through the camper to the rear window where I could study their determined faces. Watching them, while goose bumps covered my arms, I suddenly saw something in the spirit, the makings of a miracle. The band of marchers reminded me of Gideon's three hundred, of Joshua's trumpeting army, of King Jehoshaphat's choir. The Poles were the kind of ordinary people the Lord delights in using to accomplish extraordinary feats—simple sinners, weak and unarmed, empowered by His Holy Spirit. It was a Twentieth Century, Old Testament deliverance march of the righteous. The unbelieving world had better beware.

When I rejoined Charlie up front, I said, "Did you ever think we would live to see a march for freedom in Poland?"

"No, it's almost unbelievable. I suppose the people here have had enough of their government's harassment. War could break out at any minute."

"Did you have to say that?" There was no use trying to conceal my uneasiness from my husband.

"Well, it's possible, you know."

"Good grief, Charlie! What would we do then?" Until he mentioned it, the thought hadn't occurred to me.

"Try to get out of the country. I don't know what else we could do."

The concern in his voice reinforced my own fears so I tried to make light of the situation. "How are you at ducking bullets, husband?"

Charlie didn't laugh. "I hope it doesn't come to that."

"Let's *pray* that it doesn't," I added and we did pray more than once as we continued down the road.

Twenty-four hours later, we were on the outskirts of

Warsaw, a mere ninety miles from the Russian border. We decided to stop and phone our contact to verify the time and location of our rendezvous. John had assured us there would be no language problem.

I spotted jumbo letters on the roof of what looked like a small hotel and I pointed it out to Charlie. "They should have a telephone, eh?" I said, trying to imitate John.

Charlie smiled, then carefully maneuvered Baby Blue through the parked cars to the rear of the building where he parked and locked the cab, and I checked the camper door. We patted Baby Blue's fenders, thankful she was in such good shape, and then we strolled hand-in-hand to the hotel entrance.

The lobby was less than inspiring—not that it mattered. It felt so good to stretch and shake the stiffness out of our bodies. John had armed us with a meager supply of *zlotys* for this very occasion, but a search of Charlie's pockets produced none.

To solve the problem we approached the young woman behind the counter. She was friendly enough until Charlie requested some coins to make a phone call and shoved an American dollar bill across the counter. "Can you change this?" he asked politely.

She stiffened, shoved it back, and shook her head no.

Charlie smiled and slid it back. When she quickly slid it back to him again, I sang, "This is not getting us anywhere."

What we did not understand at the time were the serious implications of Poland's inflation problems. How could we know the devaluing Polish currency was almost worthless? It would have taken a wheelbarrow full of zlotys to exchange our American dollar. Our asking the clerk to do it for us was a social error bordering on impudence and lunacy.

I tried a new approach. "Telephone," I said a little too loudly like all Americans do when trying to communicate with a foreigner. I forgot that I was the foreigner. I mimicked making a telephone call with my right hand while pointing to the money with my left. Her expression remained stoic while she pretended to ignore me.

Finally, after becoming irritated by the episode, she yanked an ancient black rotary phone from under the shelf. I had not seen one like it in years. She placed it on the counter then handed me the receiver. I smiled and nodded a weak "Thank You," and handed it to Charlie. He dialed and soon began talking in a normal voice. "May I speak to the Padre?"

After a pause, he repeated his question louder. "Sir, is the Padre there?" He listened as our eyes met.

I guessed at what I thought might be the new problem: "Whoever that is doesn't speak English, does he?"

"No." He groaned. *Why is nothing ever easy?*

He hung up and we walked back to the camper. I checked my watch—ten minutes after one. Our appointment was for six o'clock, both knew it was time to seek the Father's guidance for our next move. So we crawled back into the camper and prayed.

Charlie was hungry. So was I. Sitting at the kitchen table sharing tuna sandwiches and the last two chocolate chip cookies, we rehearsed our memorized information. John had been specific with his instructions explaining as much as he thought wise. Within the communist political system, it was difficult to identify friends from enemies; therefore, it was vital for us to conceal the secret compartments in the camper from possibly prying eyes. Consequently, all the materials were to be transferred into large, green plastic trash bags before the drop to mislead any nosy onlookers.

"Charlie, where do think we should we go to unpack?" I asked between bites.

"I don't know," he said hesitantly. "What's the matter with doing it here? We're only a few miles from our destination."

My turn to hesitate even though I wanted the decision to be his. "Uh, nothing I guess. You don't think it will be a problem with all the people outside coming and going?" I swallowed hard. "What we're about to do might be noisy."

Charlie had decided. "We'll keep it down" he said, stuffing the last bit of sandwich into his mouth, and wiping his hands on the towel. He looked and sounded confident, and that was good enough for me. If we perish, we perish.

I cleaned up the lunch mess, shut and locked the window, and closed and clipped the drapes together to discourage prying eyes, while Charlie shut all the vents to muffle our noise. After we sealed ourselves in, the shell quickly became an aluminum cauldron. The temperature must have reached at least 110° F. Within minutes, our clothing was dripping wet. Sweat ran down our foreheads in rivulets. The hot air made breathing difficult, and we wondered if we would suffocate before completing our task.

While Charlie changed into a pair of shorts, I pulled the slippery plastic bags out from under the mattress. My Charlie is a big man, and for him to squeeze into position to empty the compartments was a struggle. Finally, after several grunts and groans he reached the inside latch that stuck like glue. He tried pulling it from different angles, but without success. Poor Charlie!

Then we heard footsteps coming toward us. We froze listening. I lifted the corner of the curtain and peeked out. Three people walked by on their way to the hotel. *Were we becoming paranoid?* I looked over at Charlie and sighed. When the footsteps faded, I checked again but this time saw no one.

We turned our attention back to the unyielding lid. Charlie shifted his body into a different position, braced himself and yanked with all his might. The top came loose in his hand and he plunged backward, bouncing off the kitchen counter and landing on the floor with a thud.

I panicked. I whispered, "Honey, are you all right?"

He sat up and rubbed his head. Silently, I joined him on the floor and we stared into the opening. There they were, stacks and more stacks of black Bibles. Russian Bibles. What a thrilling sight. Glory bumps covered me from head to toe. God's promises recorded on those very pages—foolishness to unbelievers; to us who believe, the power of God and the promise of eternal life.

We sat there and stared in awe. Mysteries, first hidden for centuries, then forbidden in Russia for almost seventy miserable years, were waiting there before us, ready for eager hands, free for the taking. God was offering them to the simple and the wise, the poor and rich alike, the weak as well as the strong. All who would search their pages for truth and meaning to life, would find it. My heart leapt at the prospect.

O God, what is man that You are mindful of him, and the Son of man that You care for him?

"Charlie," I whispered, "just think of the chain of people making this project possible—those who gave money, the translators, the printers and book binders, John and now us and who next? Whew! Only God knows." And I wondered, *Whose hands will hold these books next? How many lives will they change? How many will hear the call to preach because he received one of these Bibles?* The possibilities were endless. *Thank You, God, for letting us share in Your miracle.*

Charlie grinned and gave me a meaningful wink. Yes, we both understood the eternal implications of what we were about to do. But first, the compartment must be emptied, the Bibles repacked into the plastic bags, the delivery made, and for us to survive long enough to move on to the next episode.

Silently, humbly, urgently, we began our labor of love. Charlie tugged at two books jammed near the top. Unexpectedly, they came loose, releasing the others, and they all came tumbling down, landing on the floor one pile after another, making a terrible noise.

We gasped, then froze, gazing deeply into one another's eyes, wondering if the racket would alert the wrong people. Did

I hear footsteps outside the window? Yes. Was this the end of the line for us? We remained locked in fear, listening to the sound approaching. I stopped breathing. They came closer, up to the van, then they too passed by and faded into the distance. I gasped for air, then shook off the fear, because there was no time to lose. We grabbed and stuffed, and finished the job, ready to leave only a few minutes behind schedule. It was a miracle.

With only a few miles to go, Charlie navigated as I drove out of the parking lot then turned west down a tree lined street. Traffic was moderate when I began a left hand turn from the middle of an intersection. Then the driver in the car behind me blared his horn.

"What?" I said to Charlie, slamming on my brakes, making a dreadful screech as we came to a sudden stop. "What does he want? Does he want me to stop? Does he want me to hurry?" I said, starting to accelerate. But a driver was coming at me from the opposite direction, yelling at me in Polish. I was frantic. What was going on? What was I doing wrong?

Again, I slammed on the brakes, noticing that pedestrians were crowding around to investigate the commotion. Within minutes, a frowning policeman appeared on the scene and signaled me over to the side of the road out of the way of traffic.

Bewildered by the turmoil, I whimpered to Charlie, "What did I do?"

"I think we both did it. I think this is a one way street."

"Oh no," I groaned. "I bet you're right." What disastrous timing for such a stupid mistake.

As the officer approached me, I glanced over my shoulder at our huge plastic trash bags bulging with contraband, and felt a blow to the stomach. Anything was possible.

The officer yelled at me in Polish and, of course, I could not understand him. *God, what should I do?* I had to appease him somehow before he decided to snoop inside the camper and maybe even check out our immense load of wanted "garbage."

I flipped my palms up and shrugged my shoulders, trying to appear calm. He glared at me, then walked around to aim his diatribe at Charlie who was also at a loss. Suddenly, I had an entertaining thought, maybe an answer to my prayer: *Is that You, God? Could it be that You sometimes condone bribery?*

I remembered reading about Rahab and how she lied to protect the spies on God's agenda. As much as I hated the idea, I resolved to offer the officer a bribe. It was risky but, if I had guessed correctly, he would take the money and go about his business elsewhere. On the other hand, if I was wrong, I had just slammed the doors on our separate prison cells. It was a gamble either way, but one I felt we had to take.

I dug through my wallet and pulled out a nice green unmistakable US one dollar bill. His whole face lit up with a big toothy smile. He nodded his approval then suddenly became quiet, until Charlie shoved the money through the window. The officer grabbed it out of his hand, stuffed it into his pocket. Then he just stood there staring at us. What was he thinking? Did he want more? How much more? What was the penalty for bribing an officer in Poland?

O God, what have I done? I prayed silently, while he stared at Charlie who stared straight ahead. We waited. No one spoke, and finally the officer growled, turned on his heels, and stomped off.

As soon as he was out of earshot, Charlie and I exhaled a simultaneous and equally loud and long, "Whew!" What next before we reached our appointed rendezvous only a few miles away?

According to John's directions, we were to turn left at a big oak tree onto a narrow dirt road. At least that's what I recalled. Charlie, on the other hand, thought we were to turn right onto a paved street not too far beyond a railroad track. We were three days and eleven hundred miles away from the ashes of our burned instructions in West Germany, and we each remembered something different. And the clocked ticked on. What should we do?

Charlie suggested that we continue in the same direction while seeking the leading of the Holy Spirit, Who certainly remembered the instructions even if we did not. I agreed since we obviously had no other options.

Then on the left I spotted a tall oak tree. Its leafy branches signaled to us like a lighthouse at the entrance through a treacherous shoal. We grinned at each other. Victory was ours.

I swung Baby Blue wide on the left turn and we started bouncing down the dirt road, slowing our speed as the potholes became deeper and more frequent. Low hanging branches slapped across the windshield and tall weeds scraped the doors on both sides. With all the shaking and rattling, I could barely hold the steering wheel steady. The old Ford began sounding like a bucket of loose bolts.

The firm dirt soon became soft sand and our traction became sluggish, like the wheels were sinking. The thick dust kicked up behind threatening to engulf us. No one ever said this was going to be easy! Even so, if it didn't get any worse, we would keep on going. But it did get worse. Finally, the road ended at a narrow path.

"This can't be right," Charlie said. "We're not supposed to blaze our own trail."

I squinted through the shadowy thicket ahead of us and said, "Well, maybe I can back out."

"Wait a minute," Charlie said. "I think I see something up ahead, a shack. Looks like it's abandoned, but you can probably turn around in the yard."

"Good thinking! Turning around would certainly be easier than backing up." I shifted gears, and Baby Blue waddled and crept and crunched through the undergrowth into a fairly open area closer to the decrepit old building. Charlie got out to clear away a couple fallen branches and guide me so the wheels would not get stuck in the soft earth.

He was in front of the truck walking backwards and guiding

me with hand-signals. "Okay," he said calmly, "over this way, go slow . . ."

Suddenly, from behind the shack three dogs the size of German shepherds with the pale eyes of Malamutes and the meanness of Dobermans came charging out at a silent dead run straight for Charlie.

I screamed. "Charles! Watch out! Behind you!"

Charlie whirled around and set off their wild, ferocious yelping and barking. Charlie never moved so fast, and was only a few feet ahead of them when he jumped inside the cab, and slammed the door just in the nick of time.

"Dear God that was close! Are you okay?" I blurted out my concern and reached for his arm.

Charlie was speechless, panting, visibly shaken, as he looked out at the mangy mongrels leaping at his window, scraping their nails on the door, and slobbering on the glass. "That was too close!" he stammered.

The dogs stood off a few feet snarling and barking fiercely. Their message needed no interpretation: We were not welcome there. Forget about turning around! I shifted into reverse and began creeping backward judging distances through the side mirrors, while tears of fear partially blinded me, and the snapping canines continued to trail us barking, snarling, and flashing their teeth. It took me twenty minutes to go less than the distance of two city blocks but we made it back out to the main road. So much for the "dirt road next to the big oak tree"!

Back on the highway, I drove on feeling like a soldier charging straight into an ambush. But as soon as Baby Blue bounced over some railroad tracks and we entered into a small town, I spotted a cross rising high into the overcast sky.

"Over there behind those trees!" I shouted. "Charlie, do you see what I see? That must be it!" Our spirits rose with a renewed level of excitement, and I pushed down on the gas pedal, straining the old motor. Our destination stood in the

72

middle of the next block. Now our rendezvous was only minutes away.

Immediately, people began appearing from nowhere, all stopping to gape at the monster in their midst, our beloved Baby Blue. We were getting close when I saw the beautiful sanctuary draped with red flags. I gasped! The building we were approaching so confidently served as the local communist party headquarters, not a gathering place for saints, but a gathering place for comrades! The Church's place of worship had been stolen by atheist officials to practice their anti-God religion of hate.

How disheartening! Since we didn't know what else to do, we passed by without having any destination in mind, except away from there fast.

After driving a few more aimless miles further down the road I became suspicious of a white coupe in the rearview mirror. It had been more or less tailgating us. I mentioned it to Charlie who peered into his side mirror and watched the car for awhile.

"Let's check him out," Charlie said. "Speed up a little, then slow down and see what he does." I sped up; he sped up. I slowed; he slowed. My nerves were again on edge when Charlie said, "I think we are being followed, Chop. Just don't panic, whatever you do." He kept watching the car. "I wonder who would follow us, unless . . . "

"Unless what?"

"Never mind, just keep driving. Act nonchalant."

St-st-stay calm, st-st-stay calm, I told myself. *Act n-n-n-nonchala-lant!* The driver continued riding my bumper for several more miles before making his move. He pulled into the passing lane next to us. When his front fender was parallel with ours, he motioned for me to pull over. Charlie acknowledged his instructions with a feeble wave, and we rolled to a stop off the pavement.

Sweat poured from the palms of my hands that were locked around the steering wheel like a vise. I checked out my partner who looked like I felt. *Now what?* I thought to myself. My heart pounded as I watched the stranger get out of his car. He was a handsome man, well dressed in casual clothes, at least not in uniform! I wondered, *Is he a member of the secret police doing a spot check? If so, how do we explain why we're here, two Americans in our outlandish "mobile home," roaming the Polish countryside with garbage bags full of contraband? Oh Lord, where are You? Does Your promise never to leave us or forsake us still hold?* "Charlie, what should we do, get out or stay in the truck?"

"Let's get out," he muttered in disgust.

Reluctantly, we climbed out of the truck and walked toward the man as he walked toward us. Within seconds, we were face-to-face.

He spoke quietly in perfect English. "Are you lost?" Charlie and I stared at him like deaf mutes. "If you are lost, perhaps I can help you."

We stood there speechless, and I thought, *Charlie, say something! Anything! He'll think we're idiots!*

The man repeated his question with a smile. "Are you lost? Do you need my help?"

I could not find my voice. I looked away and started coughing, thinking, *Why doesn't this man identify himself? But since when do communist cops have gentle voices and nice smiles!*

Charlie took a chance and broke his silence. "Well, uh," he stammered, "we're uh, what I mean is that we're really looking for um," then he blurted it out, "for a school for priests."

"Ah yes, I know where that is. Follow me!" he said and headed for his car.

Had the kind stranger's attitude changed, or was it my imagination that his offer sounded more like an order? Why should we follow a stranger's orders unless he was taking us to jail? Did we dare trust him? But, what were our options? We were totally confused yet we had to do something. There was a fifty-fifty chance that the man's motives were pure and we had no other way to remedy our situation except to believe that God was still in control.

"Come on, Chop. I'll drive," Charlie said out of the blue, as though he had just received a revelation.

I flashed him a worried frown, "Are you sure?"

"I'm sure. Come on, it's getting late. We'll be all right." Charlie smiled, and I suspected that my husband had heard from the Lord.

We followed the white coupe for a mile or so until another cross appeared in the distance. As we approached, the mysterious stranger beeped his horn and pointed to it. Charlie waved as our escort drove away, and we turned right onto a paved road.

Charlie raised an eyebrow and looked over at me out of the corner of his eye. "Chop," he said, "do you know what I think?"

"No, I don't," I answered him with a puzzled expression.

"I believe we just met an angel." He kept looking straight ahead and I thought maybe, I heard him wrong. "Did you say an angel?" I asked.

"I did, one sent straight from the throne of grace."

The very thought of having been in the presence of a celestial being and under his divine guidance thrilled my soul. I was speechless.

Charlie made a right turn onto an unpaved driveway leading directly to the church. About halfway he noticed that the gas gauge registered close to empty, but there was nothing we could do about it then.

The drive ended at an empty parking lot enclosed by a low stone wall. Charlie parked as close as possible to the three-story, red brick building that adjoined the church sanctuary to avoid becoming conspicuous. No one was in sight when we crossed through the courtyard to the rear entrance.

The portal was sheltered by a thick, green vine that climbed and wrapped itself around a wooden lattice. We stood underneath it in the cool shade while Charlie pressed the buzzer. The sound of footsteps told us that someone was coming and then the heavy wooden door opened a crack, revealing a large Polish woman standing behind it. She peered out at us for a moment, then flung the door wide and exclaimed, "You are the Americans. Welcome!" Her English was a blessed surprise.

Our Polish contact invited us inside and introduced herself simply as Mary, the housekeeper. Mary's long gray homespun dress and pale skin were brightened by her pleasant smile and lively blue eyes. Words such as character, strength, nobility and warmth immediately came to mind when she took my hand. According to John, Mary was the Padre's valuable assistant and we understood the treasures we brought would remain in her safekeeping until the believers from the Soviet Union came to retrieve them. First impressions are usually accurate, so they say, and Mary certainly made a very good one.

Mary offered little information about herself, and we hesitated to ask questions. The mission worked on a "need to know" basis, that way, if anyone were caught, there would be less jeopardy for all. The less we knew the better.

Mary showed us to the basement where the books would be temporarily stored. Now it was time to return to the truck and retrieve the bags. I felt nervous, slightly panicky so Charlie scouted out the area to make sure no one was hanging around before we stepped back out into the bright sunlight. Because of the stone wall, it was impossible to park Baby Blue next to the door and avoid the trek across the courtyard. And even though my heart was in it, hauling the heavy bags of contraband thirty yards back and forth across the lot to stash them in a secret hideaway was not exactly what I wanted to do in broad daylight.

Trailing about two steps behind my husband, I commented, "Honestly Charlie, I don't think I'm cut out for this."

He laughed out loud. "Who is? Not me! The only person I know born with enough courage to smuggle is Brother Andrew."

"Hm, well I wonder what he's doing at the moment. Never mind. I'm not complaining it's just that . . ."

Charlie stopped when we reached the camper and turned to me. "I know," he said gently. "I understand. You're nervous. And for what it's worth, so am I."

Charlie unlocked the door and dragged the heavy bags out as far as the back ledge. Hauling them in would be a two man job. I was the second man. He grabbed the front of one of them and lifted it up so I could get a hold on the back end; then we hauled them in between us like corpses in body bags. Five trips later we finished the last one, overjoyed by a tremendous sense of relief and accomplishment.

When the unloading was completed, Mary immediately double locked the door to the cellar, jiggling it back and forth to be sure it could not be opened without her keys and her knowledge. Then she graciously invited us to stay for dinner, and we readily accepted.

We followed her upstairs to an old apartment over the church sanctuary in dire need of repair. Large brown blotches on the ceiling revealed that the roof leaked. Fading walls marred by long vertical cracks in the plaster cried out for repair and fresh paint. Her few pieces of furniture were sturdy but old. Except for a gorgeous, hand painted porcelain clock adorning the middle of an old oak bureau, the entire apartment was dark and drab. When the clock chimed, the melodic sounds dispelled much of the gloom.

Mary hustled off to the kitchen after inviting us to make ourselves at home. Charlie and I had just gotten comfortable on the divan, when she returned with a tray of homemade bread, several thin slices of yellow cheese and a tiny pot of marvelous coffee which she placed before us on the coffee table.

Mary smiled warmly as I scanned the goodies. Immediately, I recalled John's remark about the price of cheese, how it had risen from 20 zlotys to hundreds in only one day. Charlie and I exchanged glances when Mary pushed the tray toward us, insisting that we eat. It might have been all the food she had but she was so gracious that we didn't want to insult her generosity. We nibbled on the cheese, sipped the divine coffee, and gorged on the delicious bread. All and all it was a wonderful meal.

"Mary, how did you recognize us as Americans when you answered the door?" I asked hoping to satisfy my curiosity.

"You stand and walk like free people." She said after some hesitation and her response surprised and humbled us.

After a few seconds of silence Charlie complimented her on her excellent command of English, and she blushed rosy red with delight. She explained how she had lived with her brother in America and stayed long enough to earn the money to buy a car for her son Alexander, who worked in Warsaw.

She had surprised me again. "Why did you come back? Didn't you enjoy our life-style and living in the United States?"

"No, not really. You Americans have everything, everything except peace and contentment."

To some extent, I had to agree with her. *We are so blessed with material goods that we often let the simple pleasures of life escape us. Clearly, America was not the same as envisioned by our Founding Fathers. When had we allowed the gods of materialism and amusement to take dominion over our souls? And how long will the Lord hold back His judgment from our nation that now winks at the two crimes He abhors the most, sodomy and the shedding of innocent blood?* I found it difficult to answer my own questions.

Charlie stood as Mary reached for my hand with something on her heart. "Dear Alyce, dear Charles," she said, "must you leave? Can you not stay long enough to meet the people who will receive the books? They so much appreciate what you have done, all you have risked for them." Then, sensing my uneasiness, she continued. "Well, even if you have to go, I want to thank you for them." She paused, looking deep into my eyes, squeezed my hand, then straightened up. "And thank you from me because they are my friends and I know how much the books mean to them."

A big man startled us by appearing in the doorway. He spoke to Mary furiously in Polish and we did not need to understand the language to know he was not bringing good news.

Mary interpreted. Moscow was putting the squeeze on *perestroika* in Poland by shutting down the gasoline pumps. She said, "My son Alexander tells me that gas stations all over town are closing. If you are hoping to get out of Poland tonight, you must go now." She looked at Charlie. "Do you have enough gas?"

"We're almost on empty."

Mary motioned to Alexander to retrieve their gas cans from a closet. "We will go to the black market. How much will you need?"

Charlie looked sheepishly at the two five-gallon cans, embarrassed at having to admit that we needed more than five times that much.

Mary's son returned the cans to the closet, and ordered us to follow him. Mary interpreted the order, then said; "Do what he says. He will take you where you must go."

We chased after Alexander at a dead run. I was breathless as we climbed into our accustomed seats and sped down the driveway after him.

Alexander led us straight into a snarled traffic jam. From every direction darting cars tried to escape the confusion. People queued up for miles to buy enough fuel to at least keep their lives moving for now. We were driving by a long line of cars waiting to get into one of the few gas stations still open when Alexander motioned for us to cut in. We followed his instructions, waved to him and watched as he drove away.

A kindhearted soul, grinning and pointing to our Florida license plate, opened up a space for me to ease our outlandish contraption in front of him.

"Another angel, Charlie?"

"Could be."

We inched along praying there would still be fuel left when we had our turn at the pumps. It promised to be a long wait. Darkness had fallen by the time we pulled up and Charlie handed over our remaining petrol coupons which were enough to fill both tanks. Sadly, the hassled, exhausted attendant pumping the gas refused them. He held up two fingers: Two coupons was all he could accept from a single customer. Two coupons worth of gas would definitely not get us to the border.

As I watched the frustrating scene unfold, a recent episode jogged my memory and I reached into my handbag for what I thought might be the magic solution to the problem. "Charlie!" I shouted holding up another US dollar bill for them both to see. The young man's face lit up as he nodded his approval, reached for the remaining coupons and our American money then filled the tanks. Now we knew how to buy all the gas we needed.

Our assignment in Poland was over. By now, Baby Blue and I were good friends. I had pushed her hard, and she had responded well.

In spite of the fact that we were eager to escape the evil clutches of communism and deliver her to the free world where she belonged, we remembered John's suggestion that we take an extra day and detour through East Germany. We decided to do it. As tired as we were, how could we miss the opportunity to see historic Berlin and the infamous Berlin Wall? We could not.

The long straight flat road seemed endless before we finally reached the West German border. American troops had been stationed in Germany for years, and I expected their influence to have converted the entire nation into a mini USA. Not so! Germany retained a strong sense of nationalism as I would soon discover at the Visitors' Bureau. I was only trying to be friendly when I blithely remarked "I suppose everyone here speaks English?"

The agent, who was not amused, answered me in no uncertain terms: "Nein, Fräulein! Dis is not America! Dis is Germany. Ve speak German in our country."

While the agent was straightening me out, Charlie was collecting brochures to take home with us. We decided to stay only long enough to see the Wall and the city, no longer, and we splurged on a comfortable hotel to compensate for our nights in the camper.

Our room was clean and small but there was plenty of hot water. I sat on the edge of the bed studying the brochures while Charlie telephoned John in Holland. To keep the cost down, he kept the conversation short. "We delivered the 'bread' to your sister," he reported and John was both pleased and relieved.

Our official mission was over and later that afternoon, Charlie and I decided to leave Baby Blue in the hotel parking lot to take the train across the border. We set out primed for an interesting little visit but instead of walking toward the station, we went the wrong way. In no time at all we were lost. Everyone we asked for directions gave us the same dire warning: "Today is not a good day to visit East Berlin."

The way they made it sound, *no day* was a good day to visit East Berlin. We momentarily considered giving up the idea of investigating on our own but then decided there was only one way to find out what life was really like on the other side of the wall. We would go.

We found the station at last and climbed the stairs to the

platform where a few people were waiting for the train. While Charlie purchased two round-trip tickets, I scanned the headlines at the newspaper stand nearby. Soon, Charlie was reading over my shoulder about the thousands of Chinese students demonstrating in the face of the Red Chinese authorities in Tiananmen Square. Neither of us could believe it. What would happen to them?

We knew the democracy movement was sweeping across the entire world like a gigantic tidal wave, but in China? We hoped it meant good news since our itinerary included a Bible delivery to the Chinese believers before our return home.

Soon, the long silver "iron horse" pulled into the station. The doors flung open and we squeezed into the crowded car. Five stops later, an East German guard boarded and stood next to me. I stiffened. His expressionless face reminded me of the Polish traffic cop in Warsaw who accepted my first bribe. After recalling that incident, I focused my attention in the other direction.

"Next stop, East Berlin." Peering through the window, we could see the ugly Wall as we passed it. My stomach knotted, remembering having read that Stalin fully expected opposition from the Allies when he first threatened to erect the Wall. He was amazed and amused that no one ever moved to stop him.

The train quickly pulled to an abrupt stop and again we were at the mercy of "Big Brother." Jammed together people inched their way down the steps to the street level. I glanced up. On the platforms above us, with loaded rifles poised, stood the communist soldiers flanked by alert police dogs. I felt as though we had entered into a deeper dimension of evil, closer than ever to Satan's power base. If tyranny had a face, it lived and breathed in this place.

"Let's go home, Chop," Charlie said and pulled me closer to his side.

I nodded in agreement. Neither of us could stand breathing

the demonic atmosphere. Charlie led the way and we made one giant loop around the station, returning to West Berlin on the next outbound train. We returned to freedom and fresh air.

The next day, we agreed to try again. We especially wanted to visit the Pergamum Museum, and decided to take a bus tour escorted by an official government guide. When our chartered coach passed through Checkpoint Charlie, it stopped to let an East German guard on board. The sight of him brought back temporary indigestion. Keeping his hand on his pistol, he walked down the aisle, pausing at every seat, and scrutinizing every passenger. He looked like a man ready to shoot. No one dared challenge his authority.

Charlie pointed to the guards standing next to the bus with more trained dogs. I watched the men as they slid a mirror mounted on a trolley under the frame of our bus. The contraption would easily expose anyone clinging to the bottom of the chassis.

When the masters of fear and intimidation finished all the necessary rigmarole of checking passports and asking questions, we began our tour of the city. Many buildings destroyed by Allied bombers during W.W.II had been rebuilt. The city looked much better than I had expected. Miraculously, most of the museums had been spared and were still intact.

Our guide was a strange looking woman worthy of a little study. Her carrot-red hair with its purplish tinge was a phenomenon to me. I wondered if she applied her makeup with a paint roller. Her dress was inappropriately Western, a mini skirt and black blazer with shoulder padding for two, like something left over from the California of the Sixties. Her imaginative description of life in the communist state was enough to make one either snort or regurgitate. According to her propaganda, every communist is healthy, wealthy, wise and content. Paradise Lost had been found. Everyone, of course, longed to live in East Berlin but only the chosen few were that blessed. And I thought,

Come on, lady! Gimme a break!

Once inside the Pergamum Museum, our tour group split up. Taking advantage of the confusion, Charlie and I sneaked off by ourselves.

"Charlie," I said, "that was too easy. How come they let us go off alone?"

"Don't kid yourself," he said. "They're still watching us."

"Whatever," I mumbled. "Let's just make sure we get back with our group before they leave us in here overnight. Meanwhile, let's go find something—anything that has spiritual overtones."

After wandering around a bit, we entered a room dominated by massive cobalt blue walls, the authentic blue walls from the Great Babylon of the Old Testament. German excavators had unearthed the find and they kept it on display. It was awesome. The glazed ceramic tiles reached upward and towered over us. Gold hand painted images of ferocious lions with thick manes rimmed the bottom. The original Persian builders had even dedicated one entire wall to the recorded instructions on how to assemble, disassemble and reconstruct the engineering marvel.

In my mind, I conjured up the scene that took place thousands of years earlier. I pictured jeering crowds taunting the humiliated Hebrew children as they marched in disgrace through these monuments to Babylonian supremacy. God chastened His beloved Chosen People for having followed a series of evil kings and had commanded that they submit to their enemies the Babylonians. In this instance, He even called the pagan King Nebuchadnezzar, His servant. He had surrendered the reflection of His glory into the hands of His enemies. What a tragic, humbling record of failure and national disobedience sprouting from roots deep in the hearts of individual men. Charlie and I left the place saddened but glad to return to West Germany to prepare for our next adventure.

With our sojourn in Germany over, we turned Baby Blue's hood west, and began our trek back to Holland, secure in God's unending and irresistible love as proven by the demonstrations of his power and grace in our behalf. Our joy overflowed. We had no way of counting the number of lives we had touched indirectly with the Gospel, or how God would use the power of "the bread" we had been privileged to deliver.

One thing remained certain. We were changed. We had grown through what our eyes had seen. We had a renewed appreciation of our national freedoms at home—freedom of religion, freedom of speech, freedom to complain. We had loved the Lord Jesus before but now we worshipped Him even more.

Seeing John standing in the mission parking lot when we pulled in was a sight for our longing eyes. Obviously, the feeling was mutual. "My friends, my friends!" he cried out, with his hugging arms outstretched to embrace his two worn-out adventurers. "How did your trip go? But, you will tell me all about it later, eh? I have wonderful news to share with you. The mission is sending me with you to Leningrad. So, we will now be traveling together, eh?"

Such wonderful, exciting news brought tears to my eyes. Charlie grinned wide as the three of us hugged each other in mutual affection.

Across the USSR, *glasnost* and *perestroika* were becoming household words. Openness, freedom of speech, change—it all sounded too good to be true. After all, the Soviet Union was still entrenched in communism. Anything could happen, and probably would.

5
Dutch Encounter

Our enlightening conversation with John ended and now it was time to get to work. A firm spray of cold water spewed from the hose Charlie was holding and washed all the mud off Baby Blue's exterior. Meanwhile, the unmistakable hum of the vacuum I was using inside reminded me of home. It took quite awhile before we finished and then made a slow, careful, last minute check just in case we missed anything. We hadn't, our Baby Blue was clean inside and out. In seven days, we had added twenty two hundred miles to her odometer and a new taste of eternity to our own lives. After what we had been through together, I had mixed feelings when we left the garage and went inside the office to turn in the keys. John met us in the hallway and after a few minutes of chitchat encouraged us to take another day off to enjoy some rest and relaxation which sounded like a wonderful idea.

After a good night's sleep, we got an early start the following morning and immediately purchased two first-class tickets for the train to Amsterdam. I was especially eager to see and experience the city that was fast becoming known as the melting pot of Europe.

Charlie, however, simply regarded Amsterdam as another spreading metropolis with serious, bizarre, internal, big city problems. But as usual I was brimming with anticipation.

Fortunately, my patient husband had grown accustomed to my spurts of enthusiasm and endured my brisk chatter with our neighbors in the coach by nodding his occasional agreement.

The train pulled into the station and a steady flow of travelers swept us along through the busy main terminal until we reached the outside. Adjacent to the entrance was a large plaza, a gathering place for a peculiar assortment of individuals, not your everyday type of common folk—weird to understate our impressions. Charlie held tightly to my hand as we moved through them. They reeked with the stench of marijuana—punk rockers with short, stiff, long spiked wild haircuts, making the simple Iroquois Indian brush cut appear conservative by comparison. The oddly arranged rips in their pants looked deliberately planned and I wondered about the indecipherable symbols painted all over their ragged tee shirts. I expected dirty jeans but had never before seen feathered earrings or engineers' boots decorated with chains wrapped around the ankles.

We wove though the maze of radical and diverse amateur performers who had adapted the square to host a universal curtain call. Curious about what was going on, I pressed our way into a crowd of onlookers and stood on tiptoe to watch a skinny, young man with stringy blond hair and a bare chest swallow a flaming torch. First he danced, while swinging the red hot rod in a worshipful manner as if in a trance. Then he stopped abruptly, planted his feet firmly on his small portion of the cement stage, held the flaming torch over his head and leaned back. As he slowly lowered it toward his open mouth, the horror of it all overcame me, a youth created in the image of God . . . I could watch no longer and I turned to snuggle against my Charlie's chest.

Charlie wrapped his arms around me and pulled me away from the crowd of gawkers. We had seen enough. So far, my husband's expectations about the big city atmosphere proved quite accurate. *What a mission field for street preachers,* I thought to myself.

Charlie kept an eye peeled for pickpockets as we strolled along the streets. It seemed as though peddlers from all over the continent had come to hawk everything imaginable from drugs and sex to trinkets and drummed up causes. It was disappointing but then there were also some charming sights to contrast the depravity.

We paused atop a stone bridge and gazed at one of the many canals that formed a maze of peaceful waterways, endless avenues for the floating houses of locals and romantic boat trips for visitors. Flower shops dotted the sea of humanity with delightful, colorful, profuse islands of natural beauty. And the place teemed with outside garden cafes and scented coffee-houses.

Eventually, we made a complete circle and were back at the train station when Charlie suggested we go to Haarlem to visit the home of the late Corrie Ten Boom.

We read a book about her and her family the previous year. During the Second World War, the entire Ten Boom family had offered asylum to many Jews fleeing Nazi persecution. Corrie Ten Boom's subsequent worldwide ministry of comfort and counsel began during her incarceration in the Ravensbruk concentration camp. Hers was a compelling story and we wanted to see the museum holding the memorabilia of her life first hand. Besides, we wanted a complete change from the atmosphere we had experienced in Amsterdam.

We caught the next train to Haarlem and followed John's instructions from the terminal to the Grote Markt. From there finding the house was a simple matter of reading the map.

Twenty minutes passed before we spotted the sign in front of a modest, narrow, three-story brick building advertising "TEN BOOM WATCHES." We crossed the street, Charlie opened the front door and we stepped into a room of ticking clocks. Clocks everywhere, of every imaginable type and size surrounded us: mechanical and electrical; wall models, table models, floor models and portables; cuckoos and grandfathers.

A portly, middle-aged man wearing metal rimmed glasses, white slacks and a blue plaid shirt walked out from behind a glass display counter. He extended his hand and introduced himself as the owner and curator of the tiny, world famous Ten Boom Museum.

After shaking both our hands firmly he asked, "What brings you to Holland?" A reasonable question for foreign visitors but how do we answer. That we came to smuggle Bibles?

Charlie rescued the conversation. "We came to Haarlem especially to see this place."

"Ah," said the curator satisfied.

I decided to shift the focus onto him. "Tell us about yourself and the museum," I said.

Our host, a self-appointed "watchman on the wall," responded eagerly. He gave us a passionate account of the Gestapo raids which led to a systematic, heartless roundup of Jews and Jewish sympathizers. It was a very moving testimony. We openly admired his commitment to keep alive the memory of the Nazi atrocities. In his own way, he was contributing to the hope that this disgraceful part of history would never, ever repeat itself.

Charlie and I followed him single file up the narrow corkscrew staircase and tracked the threadbare carpet through the creaky halls. On the second floor, our guide pointed out double walls, secret panels and warning buzzers. On the third floor, in the left-hand corner of Corrie's bedroom was the actual hiding place. The area had been so perfectly disguised that we would never have found it. He reached beneath a low shelf to remove a panel, two-feet high by two-feet wide. It slid open revealing the secret room. A concealed air vent cunningly cut into the actual wall allowed air to circulate from inside the house. Food came from the Ten Booms' own table and they emptied the basin used as a toilet once a day.

My flesh recoiled at the prospect of spending days, possibly weeks crammed inside such a tiny cell and I gained a greater respect and admiration not only for the courageous Ten Boom family, each one willing to lay his life on the line but also for the victims. Civil disobedience (in obedience to God) and persecution suddenly took on a new meaning.

Our short informal tour concluded and we stopped to examine the table of memorabilia and brochures opposite the front door. I noticed a colorful tapestry made by Corrie's sister, Betsie. Red, blue, silver and gold threads formed the picture of a resplendent crown. A small sign in the corner read, "How God sees our life." Opposite it was another tapestry and instead of the front it showed the back side, a mass of tangled, loose strings that portrayed another message. The sign read "What we see." How true and how often we consider our lives confused, full of loose ends and without pattern or direction. Thank God, He knows the beginning from the end from the middle.

As we were getting ready to leave, another group of visitors arrived and I wondered if they also would sense the Holy Spirit of love and courage that had directed the lives of those who once lived there.

It was still somewhat early when we returned to Amsterdam so we thought maybe we should take advantage of the opportunity to visit the Naval Observatory. This time, however, we avoided the plaza by leaving the terminal through a side door. Our plan proved an unfortunate mistake because within a few blocks we discerned a downward drag in the feel of the neighborhood. It was almost strange and we didn't know what to think since the men we observed leaning against the doorways were all well dressed with spit-shined shoes and had cigarettes dangling from their lips. When I passed close to one, I could almost feel him undress me with his eyes.

I clung close to my husband, "Charlie were do you think we are?" I murmured after walking a short distance.

"I'm not sure," he said quietly, "but I believe this must be the infamous Red Light District people talk about."

I rolled my eyes at him. "Oh brother, you must be kidding. How did we manage to do that?"

"Beats me," he said shaking his head.

Needless to say, the area had an unsettling eerie feeling about it so we picked up our pace to avoid accidentally seeing the "working women" posing behind glass windows rimming the sidewalk. We were almost to the end of the block when my eyes wandered. I stopped, turned and came face-to-face with a woman about my age. She was draped across a lounge chair with her legs propped in an obscene position. I tried making eye contact with her but her expression and her eyes were hollow.

My heart sank. Something about her touched my spirit, maybe it was because we were part of the same generation or maybe because we had the same coloring. *What happened to her that didn't happen to me?* My feelings toward her were uncertain but it didn't matter. What did matter was how Jesus wept for her soul. I remembered Mary Magdalene and began interceding for her deliverance all the way back to the terminal.

By now it was getting late and neither Charlie nor I were in the mood for anymore sightseeing so we gave up trying to find the Naval Observatory. Instead, we boarded the next train to Zwolle. Our plans were to leave with John the next morning for Leningrad and we still had to pack. On the train ride back I could not shake the need to intercede for the young prostitute. The incident had been disturbing and it wasn't until we spotted

John parked in front of our hotel that I could release it. He wiggled out from behind the steering wheel and waited for us on the curb. "Well, did you enjoy your day of rest, eh?" he asked cheerfully.

"Hm . . ." Charlie answered.

"Yes, I suppose we did," I added. The truth but maybe not the whole truth.

"Good! Glad to hear it. Now we must prepare to leave. It will be different for you this trip. Not hundreds of Bibles this time; instead I brought them with me for you to pack into your suitcases, eh?" He opened the trunk and there they were, precious Bibles wrapped in brown paper.

Charlie asked, "How many should we take?"

"That's between you and the Lord, eh." John waited while I fingered the end of my ponytail and Charlie rubbed his chin. We were thinking.

Then John began explaining how our work in the Soviet Union involved the extensive changes taking place on the political scene. The focus of this trip shifted from delivery to current events. The people at the mission needed to know what effect the changes already had on the church at large and it was our job to find out.

Because of all the mixed propaganda circulated by the Kremlin, no one was sure what to expect at customs. The difficulties of the past could not easily be dismissed. As recently as 1987, members of John's group of "tourists" were carrying one Bible each which were confiscated. Afterward the officials detained the group seven hours and then only allowed them to enter the country under strict surveillance.

John told us why his Bible had been taken. When his guard asked whether he read Russian without thinking he answered no. His Bible, of course, was printed in Russian.

His story left us in a quandary. We knew the need inside

Russia for any religious reading material was great but how great was the risk of getting it in? We had no way of knowing or finding out.

I stood waiting for the prompting from the Holy Spirit when Charlie grabbed five books. I watched him for a few seconds then supposing that his decision was my answer, I took five, also.

Charlie groaned, "Ten books? Not very many, is it?" He sounded depressed.

"Not many, considering how far we're going," I added. John picked up on our negative attitudes and asked us one of his favorite glum conversation stoppers. "How many Bibles do you regularly give away in America?"

Sadly, the answer was very few. But we understood what he inferred by the remark: as of late, many Americans were replacing Bible teachings with situational ethics, a new value system which conveniently did away with moral standards. He knew it and we knew it. In fact, if the new wave of liberalism were to succeed, Christians might soon be considered America's most Endangered Species.

At 10:30 the next morning, we met John and his coworker in the parking lot. They quickly loaded our luggage into the van and we climbed over it getting to the back seat. As we pulled away from the curb I twisted around for a last glimpse at the hotel. So much had happened to us in such a short time. In some small way it had echoed the book of Acts. Serving the Master had come to mean so much to me that I could hardly bear for it to end. Could I possibly recapture the same thrill at home? I wasn't sure.

What was it that was so different about being here? Jesus had come to life for me more than ever before. Why? Was it because of the people and their desperate need? Was it because the unfamiliar surroundings made us totally dependent on His strength? Was it because we had watched so many impressive miracles unfold day after day? Whatever the reasons, my heart was heavy laden, almost like leaving a piece of me behind. A piece I knew I would miss.

Charlie noticed how quiet I had become and drew me close to his side. My lips began to quiver and the first teardrop in the coming deluge slid silently down my cheek.

I leaned up and whispered in my husband's ear, "Charlie, do you think God will let us come back someday?"

I looked up and saw that even my Charlie's eyes were bright with unaccustomed tears brimming close to the surface. Instead of answering, he gave me a hug of understanding and my tears began to flow.

6
Russian Rendezvous

Despite Aeroflot Airlines' impressive safety record, it was impossible for me to relax on our flight from Amsterdam to Leningrad. Someone told us that Aeroflot's policy was not to report a plane crash to the public. Obviously, that would significantly affect their statistics. After giving it some thought, we agreed that it sounded like a typical communist ploy. I never enjoyed flying even under the best of circumstances so when the wheels touched down on the runway in Leningrad, I was elated.

Charlie and I followed John's instructions to keep our distance to improve our chances of clearing customs because trouble for one usually spelled trouble for all. In order to give him enough of a head start to get deep inside the terminal we took our time leaving the plane. We planned to meet him later that evening at what John had described to us as "one of the better hotels in Leningrad." He had disappeared by the time we arrived at the customs counter. So far, everything was going according to plan. We tried to appear calm; after all, this was the friendly Russia, not stringent Czechoslovakia or intimidating East Germany. Our Bibles were loosely strewn throughout our luggage, partly concealed but not really hidden. We had no idea what to expect, whatever happened no doubt depended on the mood and temperament of the customs agent at the time.

The agent we were about to confront appeared to be an ordinary guy with straight, thinning hair slicked down, probably in his late twenties. His white shirt was too big making it bunch at the waist, the top button was missing and his navy blue pants had a sheen which usually meant they were either dirty or worn or both. He was busily rummaging through the two suitcases belonging to the couple in front of us in line when we walked up.

The process was taking longer than I thought it should and I started to ponder what we had heard about the changes inside Russia as a result of *glasnost* and *perestroika*. Reportedly, together they had replaced the Russian merry-go-round of Cold War diplomacy. Still, everyone including us harbored some suspicions about our former deadly "enemies." Had they truly changed their attitude toward capitalism? Nikita Khrushchev's 1962 threat to bury us and our children was still too recent and too raw to dismiss so easily. What about Ezekiel's prophesy in Chapter 38? Anything was possible.

The concept of communism struck me more or less as a politically correct Mafia sporting lies, fear and deception as its trademarks. Even if the Soviet leadership had truly changed for the better, I suspected there still might be more to the story than was being told. Charlie and I both believed the rumors that the same people were still in power but that only the government itself was weakening. The new openness may have transformed life for the masses to some extent but tightfisted greed, corruption and vice continued as rampant as ever. We would soon learn the truth the hard way.

The couple in front of us moved away and the agent turned his attention to us. Charlie lifted our two heavy bags up onto the counter and I began experiencing the old jitters as I watched him snap open the locks. The agent surprised us somewhat when he began rummaging through our clothes and personal items. I tried not to stare at the row of amalgam filling his front teeth and thought, *Calm down. There's nothing to worry about.* But his smile faded when he picked up one of Charlie's shirts and a Bible slid out of the sleeve and tumbled onto the counter.

He looked more intent as he dug deeper. Next came Charlie's blue jeans where I had stuffed a book into each leg. He shook them out too and stacked them on top of the first one. Now he appeared serious, replacing his congenial attitude with an enemy mentality. With fervor and determination he proceeded to ransack our luggage. I watched him and felt the blood drain from my face. When he was finished and satisfied, ten Bibles sat on the counter in a nice neat pile for all the world to see.

By then, I felt faint. Charlie's attempt to explain was dismissed with a flick of his hand which I hoped was only because the man did not understand English.

Helplessly, we watched him send a wordless signal across the way to an older man in a military uniform who immediately joined us. There was no mistaking that he was In Charge and my faith waffled between flood level and drought. As soon as I made eye contact with Charlie, I could read his mind: *We've done something really stupid this time!* And I agreed. If we had intended to hide the Bibles, we should have done a better job. But this way, our apparent attempt looked like an insult to their intelligence.

Charlie and I stood like statues while the officer picked up the Bible on top of the pile, flipped through a few pages then put it back without changing his expression. He muttered something in Russian to the agent then walked away. Time stood still while we waited for something to happen, anything!

I tried to remind myself that things were different now that there was really no need to fret. After all, we had glasnost and peristroika, right? I had read all about them in the newspapers.

Soon, the uniformed officer returned carrying a clipboard, a ledger on which he entered all the information from our passports then silently gave us a final once over. And I thought, *Good-bye, world!* But instead of any more hassle, he shoved our belongings aside and started a conversation with the couple behind us. Unsure of his approval we hesitated for a few seconds then figured that we must be free to go.

We quickly crammed all our belongings, including our Bibles, back into our suitcases. As soon as we were some distance from the counter, I leaned up to Charlie and whispered "Why do you suppose the old ogre wrote our names down?"

Charlie narrowed his eyes, grimaced and growled at me in a low tone. "Evidence, my dear. Gathering incriminating evidence against us so they can put us behind bars."

"Not funny!" I said. "You're not supposed to make jokes about something that could be serious you know."

"Oh, you worry too much Chop. Come on, it's time to get out of here."

We hauled our bags through the terminal to the exit, all the while wondering if we still might be stopped. We weren't.

Once outside, Charlie flagged down a LADA taxi, a chugging sedan shaped like a black brick with a dented front fender. It pulled to a stop in front of us and my husband flashed me a dubious look. The unusual sound coming from under the hood was definitely a clue, one that pointed to a disturbing ride ahead. Hopefully, the wheezing vehicle would keep running and not leave us stranded somewhere. The driver maintained a stoic position behind the wheel while we loaded our luggage into the trunk by ourselves then climbed into the back seat. Evidently, he didn't cater to his customers.

I handed him a brochure of the hotel with the address on the cover. He leisurely thumbed through the pages, apparently admiring the photographs, perhaps planning his own next vacation. At last, he returned it, obviously in no hurry to go anywhere.

"Charlie," I whispered, "what's with this guy? Should we apologize for disturbing him?"

Charlie whispered back. "Chop, relax. You don't understand this culture. Indifference is a way of life here. This guy is simply an *aficionado* of the proverbial communist mind set that says, 'They pretend to pay me so I pretend to work.'"

I wasn't exactly sure what he meant but the driver's glumness during the ride gave me the distinct impression that the USSR was not a happy place to spend an entire lifetime.

Twenty minutes later, the driver turned right onto an access road that was in serious disrepair and he rode the brakes while the bottom of the car chassis scraped and scratched through the dips and rises in the broken pavement. Charlie and I winced at the continuous grating from beneath us. When he gunned the motor to take a running start at an incline, the engine stalled, jerked forward and choked. It took two more tries before he made it to the top and the car rolled to a stop in front of an apparently deserted high rise.

Charlie and I compared the building with the photograph in the brochure. It was the same place all right but evidently something dreadful and dramatic had happened to alter its appearance. An earthquake, perhaps?

I made a mental note to ask John two questions: First, when was the last time he had last seen this example of "one of the better hotels in Leningrad"? And second, compared to what?

Now that it was almost time for a tip, the driver became very helpful. He popped the lid on the trunk and quickly, energetically and all by himself unloaded our bags which by then were beginning to look pretty ragged. Softhearted Charlie tipped him generously.

At the same time, an elderly bellman wearing coveralls came toward us down the sidewalk from the hotel, pushing a squeaky, wooden cart. We read the name on his badge, Sasha. Sasha welcomed us with a sad smile and a few quick nods. We returned the greeting and helped him load all our stuff onto his cart then trailed him slowly inside.

Charlie went over to the reception desk to check us in while I looked around at the lobby which reminded me of an ancient American bus terminal. As my eyes scanned the room, my hopes for a luxury suite flagged and fell.

The dun-colored, cracked linoleum floor in the lobby looked worn out and tired. It was the same vintage as the matching black plastic couches with the steel frames. Wilted indoor plants cried pitifully for their last rites. Mouse gray walls and pea-colored drapes streaked and faded by the sun blended blah with blah. The large windows desperately needed scouring to wash away the grime streaks outside and cigarette smoke residue inside—all in all, a decorator's nightmare. I could hardly wait to see our room!

Charlie beckoned and we headed for the two elevators opposite the closed gift shop. One was out of order. Why was I not surprised? Sasha punched the button and we waited—and waited while a loud rumble almost a grumble echoed distantly in the elevator shaft. Finally, a car appeared and we jammed ourselves and the cart inside, turned to face front and stared at the open grate door as the car shook and rattled on the ride up to the tenth floor. The grind of metal against metal sent shivers up and down my spine as I wondered helplessly whether the motor would seize or explode before we stopped. No elevator had ever frightened me before.

A final lurch and the car came to an abrupt halt six inches short of being level with the floor. We stepped up and out into a dimly lit hall. Imagine my surprise when I saw a clone of our tour guide from East Germany seated behind a wooden desk opposite the elevator. I wondered, *Did they both intend to end up with precisely the same shade of purple carrot red hair! On purpose? Amazing!* The clone evidently monitored all the activities on that floor, watching people as they came or went. I wondered why. Her staunch presence added to my list of doubts concerning the widely advertised new freedoms supposedly occurring in the Soviet Union.

We followed Sasha and his antique cart to our room where the stubborn lock would not cooperate with his key. With a show of determination, he jiggled it, rattled it and tried forcing it to the right to release the tumbler. The handle turned cooperatively but the bolt remained in place. Poor Sasha! He struggled with it again and again then let Charlie try. Charlie repeated the process in both directions. Nothing changed. Frustration mounted.

Sasha took over again, this time grasping the handle with both hands, rattling it back and forth with such energy, I fully expected the door to fly off its hinges. Then surprisingly, simultaneously, it simply opened. Victory restored his honor. He stood up straighter than before behind his cart waiting for us to enter the conquered room.

Suddenly, my pent-up tensions all dissolved. The fears, the frustrations, the fumbling with the lock, everything struck me as hilariously funny. I bent over double, laughing while Charlie and Sasha stared. Charlie, I knew, was embarrassed for Sasha's sake. He didn't want poor Sasha to think I was laughing at him. I wasn't, of course. I just couldn't help myself.

Tears poured down my cheeks as I stumbled into our narrow, musty room and I collapsed on the nearest bed. Hugging my middle I kept laughing like a loony leaving the men to deal with the luggage. When they were through stacking the bags inside Charlie tipped Sasha and sent him away happy.

Still laughing and wiping my eyes and blowing my nose, I turned to face the room. Even it was funny. A single, blood red drape sagged from a bent rod extending well beyond both sides of the window frame. It almost covered the one small window that gave us our only source of outside light. The carpet, of course, was brown, dark brown. Nubby, mouse gray blankets were folded neatly at the end of each little iron bed. There were no bedspreads but the sheets and pillow cases were immaculate. So was our private bathroom, a tiny room with a large lion clawed bathtub, two small bath towels and two thin wash cloths. No one could accuse management of cluttering the place with extravagant, capitalistic nonessentials. Jesus started His life in a stable so we could manage because the joy of the Lord was our strength.

A sign with a big red X across an electrical plug sat on top of the TV set. I showed it to Charlie. "What does this mean, that we can't use any electricity?" Usually, a sign with an X meant no but it was unclear "no what?"

Charlie studied it for a moment then shrugged before he answered me. "I'm not sure what it means, Chop."

He handed the sign back to me and started reading the menu from the restaurant on the fifth floor. "Come on, let's go eat!"

I hesitated because that meant another five floors down in the elevator and five floors back up. Persuasive me talked Charlie into using the stairs instead.

A disinterested maitre d' greeted us when we entered the restaurant and glanced around the large unoccupied dining room. He led us passed the empty tables to a booth by the window overlooking the beautiful Neva River. We stared at a man leaning against the wall who, we supposed, would be our waiter, hoping to attract his attention. It didn't so we read the menu again, trying to be patient until maybe the idea would occur to him that we had come to his restaurant to eat. We watched a hydrofoil zoom across the choppy water, searched the distance for another boat and scanned the room several more times for a different waiter. No second hydrofoil and still no waiter.

Since Americans tend to be a little pushy anyway, I called over to the leaning man, hoping not to annoy him too much. I didn't want to be a nuisance. I just wanted coffee. "Do you speak English?"

He answered, "No," and remained as he was.

"Coffee!" Charlie declared sharply, glaring at him while turning our cups right side up.

The waiter visibly sighed, brought over the pot and poured

coffee mostly into our cups, splashing it into our saucers then walked away. We still hadn't ordered any food but at least we had coffee.

"Charlie," I said, "I wonder how long this meal is going to take. Do you suppose, if we order pork chops, we'll have to wait while somebody goes out and kills the pig?" Charlie laughed and I took a sip of the black brew in my cup. "Yuck! Motor oil! Maybe this is a bad idea. Anyone for granola bars?"

Charlie said, "Shh!" then took a sip. "Come on, Chop it's not that bad. Don't be so finicky. The food is probably great."

"We'll see . . ."

A second waiter appeared to take our order. He didn't understand English, so we made him happy when we ordered the Special since that was the only item on the menu we could all three agree on.

Then I had a thought that rebuked me for my supercilious attitude. "Charlie," I whispered, "is it possible that since the government has made all the decisions for everyone in this country for the last seventy years that these waiters aren't lazy? I wonder if they're actually unable to decide for themselves when apathy is inappropriate?"

"Yeah, maybe you're right. How swift would we be after seventy years of having somebody do our thinking for us? Like being in prison for seventy years."

The question hung in the air, unanswerable.

It took quite awhile before our waiter returned with the first course of our dinner, cucumbers and fresh bread. I made a point of smiling when I said thank you hoping that might encourage him. He soon brought the main course and I reminded myself that we only needed to eat to remain alive not necessarily to enjoy the food. Neither of us could identify the meat but we could identify the gristle. I passed but Charlie took a few bites before he lost interest. There were also two plates of tomatoes, cabbage and greasy potatoes. We ate what we could then left the restaurant disgruntled having learned a valuable, cross-cultural maxim the hard way: Expect the worst and avoid disappointment.

Charlie and I took the stairs down to the lobby hoping to find John, who alone knew what our plans were. He had promised to be in touch as soon as possible but that was four hours ago. We were disappointed when we reached ground level and scanned the room only to discover that the lobby was empty. Uncertainty lingered in the air. Since the front door was propped open and a soft cool breeze invited us outside we decided to take an evening stroll. We checked the street in both directions. Still no John.

We meandered along the waterfront and soon came to a peaceful quiet spot. Only the soft swish of the river against the rockbound shore broke the silence. A mystical hue swathed God's handiwork in an enchanting crystalline light, neither night nor day. The priceless moment brought to my mind God's promise to Joshua when he crossed the Jordan: *Every place that the sole of your foot shall tread upon that I have given you.*

I prayed, *Father, please return this land to Your people for Your glory.*

By then, Charlie had noticed an older man with a young boy, possibly his grandson, fishing along the bank. Enthused by the prospect of having an enjoyable conversation with the locals we approached them.

"We're visiting from America," I called, trying to get their attention. There was no response so I tried again. "Hello, there! We're Americans." This time I waved. There was still no response even though I felt sure that by then they had to be aware of our presence. We were only about twenty feet away.

We were walking toward them when suddenly the old man turned and glared at me. "No bomb! No bomb!" he shouted.

I stopped short and just stood there looking at him then shook my head vigorously in agreement. "No! No bomb! No bomb!" I answered and slowly backed away. *How much anti-America propaganda did it take to convince him that Americans are war mongers?* I wondered.

The old man turned back to his fishing and we headed back to the hotel.

I tried fighting off a case of discouragement but so far the USSR was a confusing country economically, politically and spiritually. Several troublesome thoughts had me perplexed. *If the Soviet states split apart, who would gain control of their military arsenal and all their stockpiled nuclear weapons? What about Ezekiel's prophesy in Chapter 38? Would glasnost and peristroika backfire ushering in a tyrannical lunatic like Hitler, for example? Easy to believe since history has a way of repeating itself. Only time would tell.*

"Charlie, I've made up my mind. You know what I'm planning to do?" I said when we reached the lobby.

"No telling! What?" he answered with some hesitation.

"Two things: stop being friendly here because I keep getting in trouble..." (Charlie snorted.) "... and become active in politics after we get home."

My husband said, "No comment."

Even though Charlie looked as tired as I felt, he was a good sport and climbed the stairs with me. By the time we reached the tenth floor, we were both ready to keel over and he vowed never to walk up again.

In the hall I stood aside while he gave the door knob a taste of the gorilla tactics he had learned from Sasha. It worked and we stepped inside our room, drew our one drape and hurriedly readied ourselves for bed. Our joint prayer of intercession reached heaven as we spoke our dear John's name to the Father. As I dozed off, John was the last person on my mind.

The sudden, shrill jangle of the telephone alongside the bed startled us both out of deep sleep and we sat bolt upright. I turned on the light while Charlie grabbed the receiver. A brisk, argumentative exchange ended when he slammed down the receiver.

"Who was that?" I asked.

"Some guy from the blackmarket who wanted to know if I had anything to sell and wouldn't take no for an answer."

"Really? Who would be bold enough to call about that in the middle of the night?"

"Beats me!" Charlie said and I turned off the light.

We dozed, only to be awakened by a loud insistent knock on the door. I turned on the light again and said, "Maybe this time it's John."

"I hope so," Charlie answered still half asleep. He slipped into his pants and stumbled across the room, stubbing his big toe on a chair leg. When he opened the door, I could see the faint image of a man standing in the hall.

"Yes, what is it?" Charlie asked.

The man just stood there without saying a word then turned and walked away. Charlie stared after him for a minute before coming back inside.

"What did he want?" I quizzed him.

"I have no idea unless he was expecting somebody else to open the door. I've never seen him before." We were both puzzled.

"Do you think we're being watched for some reason?"

"For what reason, that we're smug . . ."

"Shush."

". . . glers?" Charlie chuckled. "I don't know. I only wish John would show up; otherwise, what do we do in the morning?"

"I don't know," I muttered.

"Well, that makes two of us."

Charlie climbed back into bed and fell asleep as soon as his head hit the pillow.

I couldn't sleep. My mind was alive with wild and crazy

thoughts, wondering whether all the disturbing events were somehow connected: The officer's recording our names at the border, our not meeting up with John yet, the rude phone call, the midnight visitor. What if the room were bugged? I tossed and turned for the rest of the night until Charlie's alarm went off. We were running out of time. We should leave for Moscow on the evening train. But without John there would be no trip because he had the tickets. No John, no trip—simple as that. Besides, we couldn't even consider leaving without him when we had no idea where to go or what to do even if we did get wherever we were supposed to go.

Some predicament!

Regardless, of our situation it was time to get up, get dressed and seek God for our next move. Instead of staying in the room to pray, we decided to have our morning devotions downstairs outside just in case, of what we weren't sure. Charlie headed for the elevator as I headed for the stairs. The heavy metal elevator door grated open as I was passing by and in the center of the car stood our beloved John.

"There you are, eh?" John smiled warmly then embraced us as we squeezed in next to him. Somehow, the elevator seemed safe with him on board like having a guardian angel in attendance.

"You weren't worried, were you!" A statement, not a question. "They detained me at the border then I had other business to attend to, eh?" The elevator ground to a halt and we stepped out. "Better we talk outside, eh?"

We stood near the river while John detailed the plans for our Bible delivery to the Russian church. When he finished, we paused to thank God for His goodness then returned to the hotel. Charlie took the elevator up while John and I climbed the stairs to meet him on the fifth floor for another "gourmet special" in the dining room. And what a pleasant surprise: Either they had another chef or we were hungrier than we thought. The food had improved, even the coffee.

When we finished eating, I decided to register my one and only complaint with John: "I hate to say it but I find Russians very unfriendly."

John shook his head. "Yah, well, you must not take it personally, Alyce. These people are fearful and with good reason, eh? Fear has dominated their lives for so many years that it will take a long, long time for them to change and be able to relax and be friendly with strangers."

"I should have guessed," I said, suddenly ashamed of my critical attitude.

"Yah, very sad, life under communism. The people have no knowledge of God, no hope, no real reason to live, eh? We forget how blessed we are to know the Savior, Who is everything we need. We forget until we see the sad results of not knowing Him reflected in the lives of others. The Russians have nothing and do not understand why they have nothing." He signaled for our check. "We should leave now. It's a long ride to the station, eh?"

John accompanied us to our room. Charlie gathered his shaving stuff from the bathroom while I packed our clothes, Bibles and remaining granola bars and asked John about the X sign on the television set.

"That's a very important warning, eh? You musk keep the set unplugged when it is not in use because sometimes they explode."

"Explode!" I exclaimed. "Explode, as in bomb?"

John frowned and nodded his head. "Yah, and kill many people. We must be very careful here about many things."

Was I surprised? No, not really.

7

Midnight Train to Moscow

After seeing the mass confusion created by the crowds of well-wishers saying their last minute good-byes at the train station's open-air platform we were glad we had followed John's advice and left the hotel early. The sky was overcast, which made the huge place appear downright dreary. We hurried just in case it started to rain and practically had to fight our way down the platform because John wanted us to stay together. It wasn't easy.

On our way to the passenger cars, we passed near the massive locomotive where the rumble from the engine was deafening. I winced and suddenly felt a headache coming on. I had no idea what to expect in Moscow and hadn't had a chance to ask Charlie's opinion but I personally was ready to leave Leningrad.

John approached the first conductor we saw and handed him our tickets to find out which car to board. Fortunately, we had stopped at the right place.

I was trailing Charlie and John, who had already climbed the few steps leading into the aisle when I decided to turn around for one last sentimental look and I almost caused a domino effect, an international incident. Just one quick reflective moment was all I wanted. But immediately behind little me came a huge, stocky woman in a big hurry. Plowing right into me, she gave me a shove and a dirty look and almost sent me sprawling. Pretending not to be affected by her overt rudeness, I grappled to stay on my feet and tried to move forward with her walking up the back of my shoes. I turned to see if she was actually doing it intentionally but she stared me down like some high-ranking party official whose authority had been challenged and continued shoving me down the middle aisle. About halfway down the car, my self control was about exhausted and I was on the verge of turning around and expressing a little American "know-how" when I spotted John and Charlie sitting in a sleeper compartment to my right. Grateful to rid myself of her and her infernal pushing, I ducked in quickly, sat down and let off some steam. "Whew!"

John reached over and patted my arm. "You are not responsible for their hardships," he said, with incredible discernment, "but some of them think you are, eh?"

I smiled feebly and took a deep breath, my first whiff of the stale remnants of cigarette smoke and body odor hanging in the air of the compartment. It was *déjè vu*, back to Poland on the afternoon Charlie shut all the vents in Baby Blue, or West Germany, when we burned the "evidence" in the sink and nearly suffocated.

When I caught my breath, Charlie asked, "You okay?"

"Yes," I said, and cleared my throat. "Stuffy in here, isn't it!"

"We already know, don't we, John?" John nodded.

"Chop," Charlie continued, "you had me worried for a minute. What happened? I thought you were right behind me?" Before I could answer, he raised one eyebrow and gave me one of his scrutinizing looks. "Come on Chopper, tell me the truth; you didn't change your mind and decide to be friendly again, did you?" He laughed.

"Not with . . ." I could feel my anger rising. "Never mind," I said. "Forget it." I looked up at the top bunk. "I guess that one's mine?"

"Well, it would be pretty hard for one of us to squeeze in up there," Charlie answered. "Uh, do you mind?"

"No, of course I don't. It's plenty big for little ol' me."

Having said that I decided to investigate while the men tried to open the window. I climbed up the wooden ladder then crawled to the center of the mattress which was as hard as a plank. When I lay flat, the ceiling was not quite two feet above my head and I had to fight off a mild attack of claustrophobia. Not one to give up easily, I shifted my body sideways to see if that might help. It didn't.

The men were having no more success with opening the window than I was having getting comfortable on the bed. By the time they gave up, they were both dripping with perspiration. John was wiping his brow with a handkerchief when he looked up at me squirming around, trying to get situated. "How is it up there, eh?" he asked, as the two of them collapsed on the bunks opposite each other.

"Just a little tight."

"Why don't you come down and sit with us for awhile," Charlie said, "It's got to be cooler down here."

I took his advice and slid down then wiggled in next to him on the bed. Suddenly, the car shifted, creaked, groaned, jerked and moved forward, swaying like a drunk until the train gathered a little speed. Charlie and I sat watching some fairly uninteresting scenery out the window while John glanced through his paperwork. Finally, after one violent lurch pitched us forward and momentarily pinned John back against the wall, the train picked up momentum and the vibration of the wheels became a hum spinning over the tracks, rhythmic almost soothing.

We continued watching the landscape whizzing by for awhile until John finished reviewing his paperwork, folded his notes in half, stuffed them into his pocket and asked Charlie, "Tell me how you found the Lord, eh?"

Charlie first gathered his thoughts, sorted them out and then he was ready. "It's difficult for me to explain unless you understand something about the way engineers think. Because of my training, it's sometimes hard for me to accept what I cannot prove. And I approached Christianity like I did everything else, like someone from the Show Me State."

"Hm," John said rubbing his chin. "You Americans have a unique way of saying things, eh? What is this Show Me State? Some kind of expression for engineers?"

Charlie answered, "Not originally. It refers to someone from Missouri, where the natives have reputations for being hard to convince. But now it refers to any skeptic, someone who has to have the facts proved so the term could apply to engineers.

My Christian boss gave me a book on Bible prophecy and insisted I read it through. I found it fascinating! He knew I would never simply take it at face value and avoided discussing it with me until I could prove or disprove it with Scripture. So of course, there was no way out for me except to compare it with the Bible. Tricky fellow, my boss."

John smiled mischievously, making me wonder if he had used the same tactics on someone else. "Apparently, your research convinced you, eh?"

"Yes, it convinced me. I read through the Bible twice. No matter how I tried, I could not disprove the prophecy. I always came up with the same conclusion that Jesus Christ of Nazareth is indeed the Son of God. And I didn't have to check my brains at the church door, as they say."

John looked confused again. "Check your brains?"

"That means, stop using my intelligence. I didn't have to accept Christ as my Savior on blind faith. And now, I'm a compulsive Bible reader. And I must admit I was very surprised to learn that the death and resurrection of Jesus Christ is and was the most widely witnessed event in world history. No

matter what the cynics claim, they cannot discredit His resurrection because no one ever found His dead body. The tomb
was empty. And certainly, the apostles would never had died
willingly as martyrs for a lie. So for me to deny His deity would
be foolishness and I'm not into foolishness."

"Yah, well, it's good that you got beyond your intellectual
pride, eh?"

I stared at John, contemplating the word he had used—
pride. *Is pride what keeps a person from Christ?* It was a
tremendous revelation for me. After a moment, I became eager
to tell about my own experience with my blessed Lord. "My
turn?"

"Yah, your turn, eh? And he gave me a reassuring smile.

"My experience was quite different from Charlie's. I was
brought up in church but never sought the Lord until I was up
to my ears in trouble, out of work, running out of money,
desperate and ready to try anything. As the person considered
by my schoolmates as most likely to succeed, I had failed big
time!"

"Big time?"

"Failed miserably. I will never forget June 4, 1980 or the
decision I made that night that changed my life forever. I had a
neighbor who kept inviting me to her church, kept telling me I
would like it, that it was nothing like any church I had ever been
in before. She kept inviting me and I kept refusing, but finally
I said okay, and one night I went alone. I sat by myself until
every spot was taken including the one next to me occupied by
an enormous guy who overflowed the seats in both directions.
He dressed in scruffy motorcycle leathers complete with
headband and scared me to death. The band was really a rock
group. When they started up, I felt like bolting for the door but
something kept me pinned to my seat and I stayed to the end.
I was fascinated with the young pastor's message, like a rerun
of my life story, trial and error, running into brick walls, running

from God. While I sat there stunned, wondering how this man knew I was in the audience, he said something that really got my attention, "Who in here has never been born again?'

"Somehow, I felt certain he was speaking directly to me. 'Born again?' No one had ever asked me that before. He said we had to repent of our sins, ask God to forgive us and be born again. I got up to leave but when the big guy next to me started down the aisle sobbing, I followed him."

I could feel my tears surfacing as I paused to let out a deep sigh and catch my breath. Neither John nor Charlie said anything, so I continued. "I didn't know what all that meant, about all the changes that God brings when we're born again by His Spirit but I do now. Like the song says, 'What a wonderful change in my life has been wrought since Jesus came into my heart!'"

Still no one spoke. It was like we were all three caught up in personal reflection. Eventually, I broke the silence when I said, "How about you, John? How did you find Jesus?"

"My experience is also quite different, eh?, because I accepted Christ as a child. But instead of talking about me, let me tell you about my friend Tahir." John retrieved a snapshot from between the pages of his Bible which he handed to Charlie, who then showed it to me. It was a picture of a young Arab, his face more rugged than handsome with black hair and a somber, faraway look in his dark eyes. After studying the picture for a few seconds, Charlie handed it back to John who tucked it carefully away before continuing his story.

"Tahir?" I asked quietly.

"Yes, someone you will spend eternity with, eh. I met Tahir last month in Iran shortly after his release from prison. A mutual friend introduced us and we spent the afternoon together. He had already been a target of prayer at the mission and I was eager to hear his testimony, much of which is not pleasant, eh. Tahir told me about being held in solitary confinement and then the beatings. They beat him many times." John paused and we could tell it was difficult for him to talk about the torture his friend had endured but he continued. "Tahir lost everything, eh? His wife, his children, his business, everything. His family were all very religious Muslims and tried three times to kill him."

I broke in. "What? His own family tried to kill him?" I was appalled.

"Yah, three times. Twice his father and brothers attacked him with knives. His mother tried to poison him. They believed they were doing Allah a favor. If it hadn't been for God's protection using Tahir's Christian pastor, they might have succeeded, eh?"

Charlie was speechless. I shook my head in dismay. "How terrible, how sad to have the people you love turn against you. How long...Oh, I can't imagine it, the poor man! Charlie, what would we do under those circumstances?" Charlie had no answer, only a shrug.

"Yah," John said, "and now after five years in prison, Tahir starts over, eh?" I saw a tears in John's eyes.

"Five years! What had he done?"

"Done? Yah well, nothing we would consider a crime, eh. He refused to deny his faith in his Lord and the government accused him of apostasy. He was never officially charged so there was no trial, eh."

I interrupted him again. "Can they do that? Imprison someone without a trial who hasn't broken any law?" John raised his eyebrows and I suddenly realized how naive my question must have sounded.

"Alyce, in Islamic countries conversion to Christianity is a crime punishable by death, depending on the country. Discrimination, imprisonment, and murder are not unusual penalties if a person is suspected of blaspheming the Prophet Mohammed, eh. It is extremely difficult for believers to keep the faith and they need our prayers." John paused and let out a deep sigh. "Yah, the church has a great challenge ahead if we are to share the Good News with the Muslims or the whole world for that matter, eh?"

Neither Charlie nor I knew what to say. What could we say? We knew nothing really about the problems facing Christians in the Middle East, even less about the solutions.

John understood our sense of helplessness. "It's getting late," he said gently, "time for sleep, eh?"

We agreed. It had been a very draining day.

Charlie boosted me up to my bunk where it took me a few minutes of rolling this way and that before I wound up lying on my back. I preferred not to sleep in my street clothes but the present arrangement ruled out changing into pajamas. I could not relax. Tahir's story haunted me. I kept seeing his face before my eyes and praying for him and others like him until I dozed off.

Within minutes, I began to dream a strange dream. I saw myself inside an enormous cathedral kneeling at the altar when I heard a crowd outside making a loud commotion. I listened for a minute, hoping, praying the noise would stop but it didn't. Somehow I knew that someone was coming to arrest me or maybe even kill me. I trembled as I waited when suddenly the back door of the sanctuary flew open. A mob of screaming Arabs poured in toward me, beating the air with their clenched fists and chanting, "God has no son! God has no son!"

Louder and louder, closer and closer they came while I lay paralyzed with fear. I could neither speak nor move. Then I remembered that there were people sitting in the balcony. Maybe they would intervene! Maybe if we all stood together we could make the lynch mob understand that I was innocent. But innocent of what? I did not know. I only knew that the people in the balcony were my only hope so with my last ounce of strength I cried out to them, "Help me! Please, for God's sake, help me!"

No one moved, no one spoke, no one did anything. They just sat there. When I looked intently at their faces, I realized their eyes were closed. Were they blind or asleep? I pleaded with them again, "Help me!"

It was no use . . . .

The nightmare ended and I woke with a start, cracking my forehead on the low ceiling. I rubbed the spot gently while muffling a groan. *It was only a dream,* I chided myself. *Thank God but what did it mean? Did the scene perhaps represent the persecuted suffering church, the sea of Islamic zealots and an apathetic world Christendom?* I couldn't be sure.

Both Charlie and John were gently snoring but I was too upset to go back to sleep and it appeared as though it would soon be light. I wondered what time it was but felt too exhausted to even look at my watch. I closed my eyes and hoped that at least I could rest for a little while longer.

The peace that comes just before dawn covered my weary body like swaddling clothes. When morning did come, I rolled over to watch the countryside fleeting by outside the window. The flat landscape dotted by rundown shacks was typical of what we had seen so far in Eastern Europe. Then I spotted a familiar sight: the old babushkas already up and working the fields. I checked on the men—still no movement. I considered giving a wake up call then decided not to. Finally, when the rural scenes began to transform into city streets, John and Charlie began to rouse. We were all hungry but they didn't serve breakfast on the train so between us we devoured all the snacks we had left except for two granola bars.

The train stopped at 10:35, right on schedule. Even though the morning was almost gone, we were still yawning when we left the station and boarded a chartered bus for the forty minute ride. I dozed all the way until the bus stopped in front of the hotel.

From the outside, the building bore a disheartening resemblance to the one in Leningrad but inside it was a hub of activity.

We checked in at the front desk and walked to our adjoining rooms on the first floor. I had a spring in my step, convinced that God does answer prayers about elevators. John left us in the hallway after explaining that he had some business to attend to. He promised to call us when he returned unless it was very late.

The room was what we expected: small, sparsely furnished but clean. I quickly took my bath (in case the hot water ran out) before surrendering the shower to Charlie. By the time we slipped our clean bodies into some clean clothes, it was almost dinnertime. Since we had the evening to ourselves, we left the hotel to explore the neighborhood.

By now the bright sunlight had softened and the temperature though still warm was comfortable. I studied the locals standing around us as we waited at the corner to cross the street. My mind tried to find a few accurate words to describe them to my friends in America. *Hearty? Persevering? Somber? Distant?* Probably all those and a few more I couldn't think of at the moment.

We began our stroll between the rows and rows of identical high rise apartments similar to the subsidized housing in our inner cities. That probably meant no souvenir shops within walking distance. Too bad!

Neither of us were hungry after our nibbling all morning but we were thirsty. After walking down a few more blocks, we approached a grocery store and decided that a couple nice, ice-cold sodas would hit the spot: Dr. Pepper, Coke, Pepsi, whatever they had on ice would be fine. We wouldn't be too particular.

The door was open, a welcoming sign and we walked in. A group of hefty women, wearing nurses' uniforms with matching white caps, were standing around idly. We smiled at them. The shelves behind the women were bare and between us stood an empty butcher case, grim reminders of the city's constant and depressing shortages. I immediately thought of the over-stocked shelves at home. "Charles," I said, "take a picture. No one at home will believe this!" Then I noticed how my voice echoed throughout the empty room. I moved to one side while Charlie focused the camera.

Without warning, one of the women sprinted from behind the counter, brandishing a broom like a sword. Apparently, she thought their national honor was at stake as she charged toward us like an angry army tank to defend it. We got the message. We left immediately with Charlie still fumbling with the lens cover.

He said, "Home, Chop!" We were still thirsty and decided the hotel restaurant might be a good choice if not our only one. The more we thought about food, the hungrier we got. We stopped by the registration desk to see if John had left us a message. He had. He had retired early and everything was okay. Good news.

We asked the clerk for directions to the restaurant. Bad news. We finally understood enough of his explanation as to why they had it closed, something to do with their plumbing backing up. The situation frustrated us until he pointed out the gift shop just down the hall.

Charlie followed me inside as I rubbed my palms together wondering where to begin. I anticipated finding at least some-thing to satisfy not only my physical thirst and appetite but also to quench my need for a shopping spree. Surely, there must be something here worth lugging home to the USA.

We hunted up one aisle and down the next, not finding much to choose from. Charlie rejected the wooden jewelry boxes I showed him because of their flimsy lids. Not to be deterred, I scrutinized an assortment of figurines, wooden carvings of little fat women stashed one inside the other. I considered buying one because I remembered they had some special significance but I couldn't recall what it was. After awhile we settled for several painted eggs and a few scarves.

Near the front was the alcohol: row after row of vodka, whiskey, liqueur and beer. Obviously, intoxicating spirits were the communists' gifts of choice. We saw no snack foods and no sodas. On that sad note our shopping excursion came to its bleak close and we went to our room to finish the remaining granola bars. I was beginning to appreciate the sustaining power of oats more and more.

Charlie and I both got a good night's sleep. When we met John in the hall the next morning, we felt refreshed but thirsty. We had already been halfway around the world since that first day we met him in his office and to think that our trip would still include a visit to Asia, took our breath away. Amazing!

Since it was Sunday, our plans included visiting a Russian Orthodox Church somewhere near the Kremlin. According to John, even though it was on the government's list of "watched churches," he still hoped to gather information there on the whereabouts of his absentee contact.

I was confident my clothes blended in with the crowd when we left the hotel. My dress was two sizes too big for me and intentionally dowdy by American standards, the perfect choice bought at a thrift shop back home for this very occasion. My shoes were flat and brown and my babushka flowered and gaudy. The overcast sky threatened rain before day's end. I was glad I remembered the umbrella. Charlie, who usually dressed a little like a French peasant anyway, had let his beard grow.

The Metro (subway) was three blocks from the hotel and I trotted along to keep up with the long legged men. It was already bustling when we arrived. John hurried us through the turnstiles then we made a dash for the down escalators. I couldn't help noticing the gorgeous ornate antique lamps adorning the center sections between the ramps. They were very unusual and I wondered why they used them in the subway station. John suggested that maybe since there was so little beauty in their lives, they did what they could with what they had.

In contrast, a life-size statue of men and women depicting the Russian Revolution across the way, loomed over the crowd. It aroused my interest but there was no time for a closer look.

We reached the platform as a loud rumble in the tunnel announced the arrival of a speeding train. It came to an abrupt stop, the doors flew open and we moved back out of the way to let the passengers out then pressed ourselves inside.

After several stops, John signaled to us that the next station was ours. We stepped off the train and followed the crowd as they rushed toward the exit. When we reached the outside, the rain had come and gone, leaving only a few puddles with the sun shining brightly. I wondered if there had been a rainbow.

Surprisingly, we seemed to be in the country. We had only gone a short distance when John stopped and pointed across an open field to a large cathedral, our destination. A narrow path cut through the low lying thicket and we had to walk single file across the field to the cobblestone parking lot. A single black coupe with large yellow fog lights was parked near the entrance to the building.

"KGB," John said. "Better we go in separately, eh? If I don't see you inside, I'll meet you tonight at the hotel." He gave us each a quick hug then sprinted on ahead. Considering the empty parking lot, it was evident that everybody but the KGB had to walk. I looked to Charlie for one of his usual comforting "it'll be all right" looks. He responded with a sideways tilt of his head, a shrug of his shoulders and a grimace. We were both scared.

We walked to the front of the building and Charlie pushed the heavy door open for me to enter first. When we stepped inside the smoky sanctuary, it was obvious the crowded service was well underway. Unwisely, I deeply inhaled. As soon as the fumes and smoke from hundreds of lit candles and burning incense hit my tender lungs, I immediately began coughing like a chain smoker. I could not stop. We had wanted to avoid being conspicuous but this coughing fit was not helping. Fortunately, no one noticed.

As soon as Charlie slipped his arm around me and asked, "Are you okay?" it calmed down some. When he held his finger to his lips and whispered "Shh," I covered my mouth with my hand and swallowed hard.

We stood in the last row scanning the congregation confident that we blended in with the parishioners. Alcoves rimmed both sides of the enormous sanctuary. There were no pews. The massive altar at the front was a maze of white marble columns, gold ornaments, icons and murals. Towering pictures of Mary and Joseph covered the walls on either side. An enormous hand painted, fifty foot high, domed ceiling depicting heaven inhabited by a host of graceful, feminine looking angels and plump little cherubs loomed overhead. The entire scene was breathtaking, very different from anything we had seen before.

The congregation faced the altar, where a white-robed priest was performing some sort of ritual. Neither of us could see very well so we quietly slipped through the reverent crowd. The sounds of whispered prayers, weeping and private devotions touched our spirits. These were truly some of God's precious people. Their every expression showed their deep love for our Blessed Lord. I smiled inwardly, thankful that God alone judges the hearts of men.

Suddenly, I began to look around. I saw no Bibles anywhere. Difficult to believe but among all those people not one had a copy of the Holy Scriptures. How sad to realize that we had brought only five from the hotel, and had given the others to John previously. So few books to meet the needs of so many! How could we know whom to give them to? We could not. Only God knew where they would be most effectively received.

Immediately, I saw a figure completely out of place, a middle-aged man wearing blue jeans and a black shirt with one foot propped up behind him, casually leaning against the wall. He reminded me of the Marlboro Man, definitely only a spectator.

John suddenly appeared next to Charlie. He handed us each a communion wafer and spoke so quietly I had to strain to hear. "I have spoken with the priest. Katyna is under house arrest."

"Will he be all right?" I asked.

"Physically, yes. But it is not possible for us to meet with him. They are watching everyone, eh?" I pointed out the man wearing a black shirt with my eyes. John knew without turning around. "KGB," he said, then added, "Be very careful here. We don't take anything for granted. These are uncertain times, eh?" He held up his communion wafer and prayed quietly, "Lord, even though we cannot outwardly share our fellowship, we partake now of Your broken body together." We paused for a moment of silent thanksgiving after our private ceremony and John slipped away.

Charlie and I had work to do too. With eyes and ears dedicated to the leading of the Holy Spirit, we had to locate the ones whom God had chosen to receive His precious Word from our hands. Almost immediately, my eyes were drawn to a man standing a few feet from us wearing a long, brown raincoat draped over his thin body like a tent. He stood just out of sight of the KGB man.

The very second I noticed him, I recalled a verse of Scripture: *My sheep hear my voice, and I know them, and they follow me.* The man's head was bowed so low that his chin and chest met and I prayed, *God, what are you trying to tell me? Is he the one?*

I nudged Charlie and he nodded his confirmation in response to my questioning look. God's prompting and my husband's agreement had settled the matter. Now if only we could pass him a book without anyone seeing . . .

We slowly maneuvered ourselves around a few people and within minutes were standing beside God's chosen vessel. I dug a Bible out of my case and waited for something to happen. I had hoped to catch his attention without being obvious but his eyes remained tightly closed. I wondered, *Now what do I do?* Then Charlie took the initiative and tapped him lightly on the shoulder. He lifted his head and stared at Charlie, who was a complete stranger to him. His expression was inscrutable, hollow, tired, weary of soul.

When I tried handing him the book he became confused, rattled, uneasy. Finally, I simply took his hand in mine, opened it and pressed the Bible into it then closed his fingers around it, giving him a reassuring smile. He pulled back, accepting it only reluctantly until he opened the cover and started to read. His eyes opened wide and he appeared stunned, realizing what it was that he held in his hand and I watched his entire countenance change.

As long as I live, I will never forget his next move. He lifted the small book it to his lips and kissed it passionately over and over while tears poured down his leathery cheeks. He then caressed it close to his heart. When the first tender moment ended, he slipped the treasure into his inside coat pocket then reached for my hands. I was speechless as he looked deep into my eyes and whispered from the depths of his soul, "Spasibo, spasibo." (Thank you, thank you.)

Apparently, no one around us had seen anything. He hugged me gently, grabbed Charlie by the shoulders and kissed him on both cheeks. Charlie stiffened at his impulsive show of affection but our Russian brother did not appear to notice and impulsively kissed us both again. Charlie suddenly handed him a second Bible, only God knew why. We could only surmise that God had a plan when he left the church immediately. Someday, we will know the results of those two little pebbles we dropped into that enormous sea of needy humanity.

Now it was Charlie's turn. He quickly heard from God and spun around to face three golden-aged, toothless saints, grandmothers standing directly behind us. He quickly dug out the last three Bibles and handed them to me with a wink and the privilege of giving them away. Trying to be inconspicuous, I offered them the books. At first, they were unsure but within seconds their happy smiles expanded into a hubbub of chatter among themselves. I watched their rising spirits with my own rising sense of insecurity, especially when they broke from their huddle and began kissing my hands, crossing themselves and genuflecting before me. I thought I would faint.

Oh God, I cried out to the Most High, *they're making a scene!*

Sure enough, curious people all around were turning to watch us. Things were suddenly out of control.

In the nick of time, Charlie came to my rescue. He grabbed my arm and swept me away from my newly-formed fan club. We were grateful they didn't follow us as we quickly slipped out the back door. As we turned around only to make sure it was shut tight, we were suddenly face-to-face with the KGB officer out for a smoke. I'm sure my eyes bulged as the second hand smoke from his lungs floated out through his heavy lips and into my face. My mouth open as I stuttered, "Uh, uh, uh."

"Excuse us!" Charlie said briskly as he pulled me past him and mumbled, "Don't look back, Chop! Just keep moving!"

We hurried across the field to the Metro station where three teenagers trying to pass for Americans greeted us. They called over to Charlie, "Hey man, you got anything to sell?"

"Nope, I sure don't," Charlie answered emphatically and kept walking.

But the leader cut us off and tried again. "Come on man, how about them shoes?" We all eye-balled Charlie's tired Reeboks. "Sixty-five dollars American, man."

"Nope, but thanks anyway," my husband said firmly.

The young man persisted. "Seventy? Seventy-five?"

"Charlie," I murmured, "that's a lot of money for those sorry puppies."

He ignored my comment, stepped around the teenage hustler and we fled down the stairs to the trains.

Twenty minutes later at our next designated stop, we returned to the street to search for our final destination, another Orthodox Church. Charlie growled at our official, downtown Moscow map that had been of very little help so far, remembering the American tour book that warned us how Russian officials switched street names regularly, to frustrate any anti-government activities by outsiders. But we had a secret weapon against their divisive scheme: It was my Charlie who was an excellent navigator with a miraculous sense of direction.

After second-guessing the map, we followed the trolley tracks to a military training facility. From there we turned left up the sidewalk running alongside a thick hedge reinforced with barbed wire which separated us from the grunts and groans coming from the recruits training on the other side.

To me, this second assignment was as unnerving as the first. John had entrusted Charlie with a confidential letter to be delivered to a priest named Dimitris. We had no specific reason to suspect the information had political ramifications but we could not be sure. But even if it had, it wouldn't change anything; we were committed and as ready as we ever would be to carrying out our assignment.

We continued on up the hill and soon a beautiful little cathedral came into view. Once again, there was only one car in the parking lot, obviously belonging to the KGB man lingering in front of the building. We spotted him right away from his new clothes and dangling cigarette. He could not have been any more obvious with a flashing neon sign around his neck.

He made my skin crawl but there was no turning back. As

my imagination tormented me with crazy thoughts, I began praying under my breath. We soon had covered the distance between us and headed for the entrance. The agent stationed himself next to the door but we casually walked past him and stepped inside.

Shrieks and wails assailed us as we entered. A funeral! *Why today, Lord?* A group of women knelt beside an open casket. I closed my eyes and exhaled deeply, hoping to release some of my fear. Their mourning was so piteous, I grabbed hold of Charlie's arm to steady myself. Oh, for a vacation from our vacation!

We saw a priest, who fit the description of our contact, kneeling at the side altar. Charlie and I moved in his direction, hoping he would acknowledge our presence. He made no move even though we felt sure he realized we were standing behind him. Bewildered, I turned my head slightly and saw that the KGB agent had followed us inside and was watching from a short distance away.

I whispered to Charlie "Guess who's here."

Charlie glanced over at him and said "Great! Just the person we wanted to see, right?"

"Right, and what do we do now? He's scrutinizing our every move."

Charlie thought a moment then came up with a strategy. "You go that way and I'll stay here," he said. "By splitting up, we force him into a decision. There's two of us but only one of him and he can't be in two places at the same time. The only question is, which one of us will he follow?"

"Since you have the letter, you make the delivery okay?"

"Okay." His face was flushed.

"If he follows me," I said, "we're in. If he stays with you, I'll come back and make a scene."

"Just come back but never mind the scene."

I paused. "Charlie, shouldn't we pray first?"

Charlie gaped at me. "No! Go now! And keep going!" He gave me a gentle shove. At the same time, the priest stood up and started walking away. Charlie followed him and I did an about-face across the sanctuary. I desperately wanted to turn around to see if the agent was behind me but I didn't dare. I remembered Charlie's order, "Go and keep going." I kept going toward the rear of the building toward a beautiful picture of Mary and the Baby. The picture became my destination. First I paused to admire it then knelt at the wooden rail. Moments later I buried my face in my hands with my eyes almost closed until I saw someone in my peripheral vision—black pants and shiny shoes, obviously the KGB agent. *Thank You, thank You, thank You, Jesus!*

I wanted to shout, Glory, Alleluia! but decided I'd better not. Instead, I looked up at him, smiled and said, "Hi!" then returned to my meditation.

A few seconds later, Charlie's hand on my shoulder startled me. "Let's go, Chop," he said, grinning. We left in a hurry and rushed back to the Metro.

We set Monday aside for sightseeing before flying out on Tuesday for China. Our contact in Hong Kong was a girl named Sharon.

8

Welcome to Asia

The next morning when I heard the alarm on Charlie's watch buzz in my ear, I cringed. *There must be some mistake,* I thought, *It can't be time to get up already! We just went to bed!* Neither of us moved during the entire thirty seconds and when it finally stopped I was grateful.

We both lay perfectly still until I could no longer resist my nagging conscience and slowly opened my eyes. *Where were we?* I couldn't remember. Nothing I saw looked familiar except my husband's sprawled out body on the other bed. I closed my eyes again hoping for a short snooze but Charlie was soon shaking my shoulder.

"Com'on Chop, wake up! You can't just lay there, you have to get with it."

"Noooo," I groaned still half asleep. I stared at the ceiling, trying to remember why I should "get with it." Oh yes, we were in the Lord's army and doing the Lord's business, that's why. Of course, Charlie was right, there was no time to waste. Our plane to Hong Kong left Moscow at noon and check-in was two hours before flight time. The airport was quite a distance from the hotel; we still had to dress, pack and say our good-byes to John. At that moment, however, I didn't even have the desire for a bicycle ride to the ice-cream store, much less a dreaded journey on a jet.

"Choppperrr . . . ," Charlie said sounding annoyed.

"Okay, okay," I sighed, rubbed my eyes and yawned.

Charlie was nearly dressed when I finally stood up and stretched my bones like a lazy cat.

It took awhile for me to get up to speed but within the hour we were downstairs with John, checked out and ready to leave. My emotions were turbulent as I watched Charlie and John load our belongings into the cab parked at the curb.

John checked his watch, "Better you go now, eh."

We stood face-to-face and I couldn't keep my chin and lower lip from quivering. "We'll keep in touch John, won't we, Charlie," I said.

"Certainly! And, John, you're always welcome in our home whenever you visit the states. We'll give you a grand tour of Southern California." Charlie gave John a brotherly clap on the back.

"Yah, well we never know what the Lord will do, eh?"

We all said "Amen" to that.

When we exchanged bear hugs with John, the tears I had held inside gushed. He gave me an understanding smile and said nothing but I still felt slightly embarrassed. After Charlie and I climbed inside the taxi John closed the door then gave the cab a tap as we pulled away.

Charlie and I watched him wave good-bye until a tour bus cut our last look at him short. I thought I saw tears in my husband's eyes when we turned around and he said "Sure going to miss him."

"I know what you mean," I answered between sniffs.

Our moods changed from sadness to melancholy and I understood the emotions attached to Charlie's next remark. "You know Chop, I can't stop thinking about that man in the church. Remember, the one we gave the Bibles to?"

"Of course, I remember."

"I've never seen anyone react like that with so much emotion. . ." His voice trailed off, he turned and stared out the window.

Charlie had drawn me into his moment of nostalgia. "Yes and what about those three dear old women in their babushkas . . ."

"And the look on that guard's face . . ."

"Which guard?"

"The one in Leningrad."

I giggled. "Yes and the KGB agent in the last church."

"I hope everything turns out for Dimitris, the priest."

"And John."

"We're definitely going to miss John."

Charlie reached over and took my hand priming my tear ducts again. "When you stop and think about it, Chop, truth really is stranger than fiction. Nobody could make up a story like this."

We finished the conversation by storing our recent memories away as treasures for a lifetime. Then our thoughts reached out for tomorrow. What new dangers would our foray into the midst of the ruthless Red China stir up? Only God knew.

The Moscow airport reminded me of LAX maybe because of its enormous size. We were becoming proficient at completing all the rigmarole involved in overseas travel and even had enough time for a quick breakfast before our departure. Charlie was ahead of me in the boarding line when the airline agent made an announcement. "Ladies and gentlemen, there will be a delay while the aircraft undergoes mechanical repairs. We apologize for the inconvenience and will be keeping you posted on our ground crews' progress."

"How frustrating," I said in a huff, "Charlie did you hear that? What now?"

"How do I know?" Charlie answered good-naturedly. "Perhaps it's only an excuse to cover up the truth." He smiled mischievously and I willingly went along with his shenanigans by asking, "Which is?"

"They're holding the aircraft because somebody's wife left their tickets at home." He laughed.

"You're not funny, Charles," I answered and rolled my eyes. I wasn't amused.

"Listen, Chop, we both know it's better to fix the problem on the ground than in the air."

I had to agree.

Charlie passed the time reading while I strolled around the terminal. Sitting for hours bothered me and I didn't want to endure any more discomfort than I had to. After all, the flight was long enough.

We boarded the plane two hours later and the aircraft was almost full when it taxied out of the gate. I had the middle seat between Charlie and a well-dressed Oriental man who sat by the window. I was busy shortening my seat belt when he glanced away from his newspaper and smiled over at us. My friendly husband took the opportunity to introduce ourselves. "We're Charlie and Alyce," he said holding out his hand.

"Thomas Li," the man responded after shaking hands with Charlie and nodding at me politely. "You enjoy Moscow?"

"It's different," I answered.

"What take you to China?"

"Hong Kong shopping, of course," Charlie gave me a peculiar look. Well, there was some truth to the statement.

"Long way just go shopping," Li remarked, "but you right. Hong Kong prices very low compared to Europe and America prices." He directed his next question to Charlie. "You businessman?"

"Yes, I work with computers. How about you?"

"Consultant for Chinese government."

"How interesting," Charlie answered and ended the

conversation by going back to paging through his magazine.

What else was there to say? We had no desire to fraternize with a consultant for Communist China's aggressively atheistic government.

The jet engines on our silver bird thrust her down the runway and within seconds we were airborne. According to Charlie's calculations, we would reach Tokyo in approximately eleven hours. Thomas Li had already returned to reading his newspaper when I leaned back, closed my eyes and hoped for the best as we soared into the distant azure sky.

I dozed off and on during the first few hours of the flight. Rest seemed much more important than snacking or watching the preview to the movie. Bedsides, I was still full from breakfast but when they started serving the main entree, I was ready to eat. The choices were between lasagna or sirloin tips, both smelled delicious. I decided to have the lasagna and Charlie settled for the sirloin tips.

By now the pungent aroma of garlic floating throughout the cabin had revived both me and my appetite. I looked up and spotted the attendants who were serving the passengers about a dozen seats ahead of us. It wouldn't be long now so I sat up straight, pulled my table down in front of me and waited. My fingers did a drum roll as I patiently watched the metal cart slowly moving in our direction. Finally, it was my turn and I gave the flight attendant an expectant grin when she handed me my tray. So far the flight had been smooth as silk.

Then the turbulence started, slowly at first. We hit a few random bumps when I began unwrapping my silverware after Charlie and I had said an inconspicuous blessing to ourselves. I glanced over at my husband who was already on his second or third bite. Not much deterred him when it came to food. I closed my eyes for a minute to try and avoid becoming anymore anxious than I already was. *Don't worry!* I scolded myself.

Determined to enjoy the meal and ignore the weather outside, I took my first bite and then another, my mouth was full when the jolts became serious. Then the seat belt lights flashed on and suddenly I wasn't hungry anymore. Disappointed, I sighed, stacked my dirty utensils on top of the plate and folded my napkin. I turned my head and peeked out the window and caught a glimpse of the dark gray curdled clouds — I withered.

The situation worsened with no sign of letting up. As the flight crew hurried through the aisles collecting the trays an announcement crackled over the intercom: "Ladies and gentlemen, this is your Captain speaking. We are encountering some turbulence because of a storm in the immediate area. Please remain in your seats with your seat belts fastened." Click.

"A storm this high? Isn't that unusual?" I asked Charlie only to have Thomas Li answer me. "No, this is season for typhoons. Legend says that every year the gods send them to warn the people," he sounded matter-of-factly.

"The gods send them?" I raised my eyebrows and gave him a peculiar look. "How interesting, do you believe that?"

"No." He folded his newspaper and looked straight ahead.

I studied him for a minute wondering what he might be thinking. His quick one word answer and stoic expression told me nothing. Since we were in for a rough flight I had to do something and the only something I knew to do was to turn to the safety of the word of God. So without thinking, I automatically dug my Bible out of the carryon and opened it to the Book of Psalms. In desperation my eyes went immediately to the verses I had highlighted in yellow.

The mighty God, even the Lord, hath spoken, and called the earth from the rising of the sun unto the going down thereof . . . Our God shall come . . . and it shall be very tempestuous round about him. Call upon me in the day of trouble; I will deliver thee, and thou shalt glorify me. (Psalms 50:1,3,15)

Thomas Li glanced over at me then murmured something again about "god." No doubt he had seen my Bible. "You are Christians?" he asked.

"Yes," I answered with a half smile, "are you?"

"No," he said swiftly only this time he sounded adamant. "Christian influence not welcome in China. Makes government officials nervous." His dark vague eyes stared into mine. "Westerners bring Bibles into country illegally. Cause many problems."

He kept staring and I squirmed in my seat. "I think I remember reading something about that," I answered then cleared my throat and tried to act natural. By then I could tell that Charlie had tuned in.

Thomas continued. "Outsiders should avoid becoming involved in Chinese politics. Bad turmoil caused by rebellious students in Tiananmen Square."

I kept quiet even though my curiosity was bubbling. I wanted to ask him what position he held in the government. Was he a member of the Public Security Bureau? Somehow, I suspected there was more to Mr. Li than met the eye.

"Chinese government punish anyone helping demonstrators," he hesitated then added briskly, "severely, with good reason, of course."

"Of course," I murmured. I could not fathom the man's character or his motives in telling me all this. Friend or foe, I was undecided. However, I was sure I did not want to continue the conversation.

The turbulence persisted and the flight attendant who had been serving us buckled herself into the jump seat behind the bulkhead across from Charlie. I interpreted her blank expression as a result of her training but after noticing her white knuckles I decided to stop looking around at other people.

Thomas had already seen my Bible and maybe I had made

a mistake by not leaving it in my carryon. I hoped not but there was no use trying to conceal anything now so I began reading where I left off. Thomas interrupted me. "In China, some say typhoon make the wicked turn to drink and the guilty turn to your God."

"Really," I said feigning interest.

After his remark, I found it hard to concentrate. Now, it wasn't only my fear of the weather that had me rattled because Thomas Li made me just as nervous.

The storm worsened. The shaking grew more and more violent. How much pounding the aircraft could take without bursting apart only God knew. Our seating section was directly over the right wing in clear view of the engines. Maybe, if we had sat somewhere else, somewhere where I could avoid watching them it might help.

Suddenly, we hit an air pocket and terror struck my heart as we plunged helplessly toward the ground. In seconds the jet fell thousands of feet before jolting to a stop in midair when I heard a sigh of relief throughout the cabin. Then without any warning another burst of air threw us upward as the plane surrendered to the mercy of the wind. The sound of someone vomiting nearby was awful. I glanced over at Charlie, his face was taut and colorless, his eyes were closed.

I looked away and buried my face in the palm of my hands. When I did the enemy assaulted my thoughts with his threats. "This plane is going to crash! You'll never get out of this alive. You fool, you should have stayed at home where you were safe."

I stiffened. *Could it be? Was this truly an ill fated-flight?*

At that precise moment, a baby nearby let out a chilling scream. I shuddered then crossed my arms and held myself. I started praying King David's words, "What time I am afraid," he said "I will trust in you." *I will trust in You, trust in You, trust in You.* I repeated the words over and over battling for my faith while hoping for a miracle.

Time crawled. Every blow to the aircraft made me wonder if it might be our last. My mind ran the gamut of verses that I had committed to memory until the captain finally announced that we were on our descent into Tokyo's Narita Airport.

"Whew! Glad this flight's almost over," Charlie commented.

"Me too," I blubbered. I was perspiring, nauseous and couldn't stop the runaway tears.

Charlie patted my leg. "Com'on, Chop, don't cry, God hasn't brought us this far to fail now."

"I know, I know," I answered with a sigh.

I spent the following moments thanking and praising God not just for what He had done but even more important for who He was. Afterward another verse crossed my mind, one I hadn't recalled before. *Would I offer the Lord that which cost me nothing.*

Clearly, King David measured the depth of his love by the depth of his sacrifice? Could I do less?

I was so relieved to be back on the ground that I almost had a hallelujah breakdown when we stepped inside the Narita terminal. The place was jammed with people and we weren't the least bit surprised when the Customer Service representative told us the airport had been closed due to weather conditions. Apparently, we were one of the last planes to land.

Charlie and I strolled around for awhile. There wasn't much to see or do or so we thought until I spotted a advertisement for the duty free shop on the lower level. After seeing the sign we immediately agreed that I would go investigate and Charlie would wait on the bench and read his photography magazine.

I must admit I was elated by the prospect of including Japan in our itinerary even if it only meant having some sort of bauble or trinket to take home with me as a keepsake. Convinced that I had come across an unplanned opportunity I trotted off toward the shop and hurried inside. I made my first pass by the display case and nearly fainted when I read the price tags. Disillusioned, I went a bit further only to find the cost of every item outrageous at least according to our budget. *I thought things were supposed to be cheaper over here,* I said to myself as I left the place disgruntled after having settled for a pack of gum.

Charlie gave me a surprised look when I came walking up. "That was fast," he said. "You couldn't have bought very much."

"You guessed that right," I complained. "Would you believe that all I could afford was a pack of gum. Everything else was too expensive. . . ."

I tore open the wrapper and handed him a piece as the boarding announcement for our next flight came over the loudspeaker.

"That's us," Charlie declared.

My shoulders stooped, my head dropped and I sighed deeply. Charlie noticed. "What's the matter, Chop?"

"Oh nothing other than I'm dreading another plane ride," I moaned.

He closed his magazine, smiled and stood. "I can't say I blame you but we can't spend the rest of our lives sitting around the Narita terminal chewing gum." He laughed.

Good ol' Charlie. I knew he was trying to be funny to make me feel better only it didn't work. I was still worried especially when I overheard a comment made by the airline agent at the gate. Evidently, the weather had lifted to some extent but we were still in for a bouncy ride. Now my mind went into a storm of its own. I couldn't take another ordeal like the one we had been through. God promised to never send us more than we could handle and I was convinced that this was more than I could handle. Fortunately for me, God agreed.

I was in line waiting for the man in front of me to clear the door to the aircraft when I felt inspired to place my hand on the outer metal. *I bring the peace of Jesus Christ to this plane,* I prayed before entering.

Amazing! Something must have happened inside of me because when I sat down next to our newly-made acquaintance Mr. Li, I felt confident of a safe journey no matter what the weather or final destination. As far as I was concerned it was a miracle.

Minutes later, we were airborne and by the time the pilot reached his cruising altitude at thirty thousand feet I was already sleeping peacefully with my head resting against Charlie's shoulder. I never budged again until our final approach to Kai Tak Airport in Hong Kong when I heard the pilot instructing the crew to prepare for landing. Time had flown by if you will excuse the pun. I leaned forward in my seat to glance out the window at the maze of concrete below. It reminded me of a giant erector set. My enthusiasm was on the rise once again.

After an unusually smooth landing I bent down to pick up my carryon. Mr. Li was deliberately staring at me. *Why did I have the feeling that he was still wondering about my Bible and what else might be in my case?*

"Enjoy your stay. . ." he said as if he wanted to say something else.

"Thanks, I'm sure we will," I answered. I purposely avoided making eye contact to conceal my uneasiness.

Charlie was standing waiting for me to go ahead of him when he said. "Maybe we'll see you again sometime, Mr. Li." And I thought uncharitably, *I hope not.*

"Wait," Thomas said a little too loudly. "Where are you staying?"

"I'm not sure . . . someone is picking us up," Charlie answered and turned to me, "Move it, Chop."

"Glad to," I said then scooted out of my seat and down the aisle to distance myself as quickly as possible from Mr. Li and his troublesome curiosity.

Hong Kong! How exciting!

When Charlie and I entered the noisy terminal I felt like a kid turned loose in a candy store. Anticipation was running high as we shuffled though the paperwork rather rapidly considering all the people and the long lines. Not having any illegal material to worry about made it much easier.

We had already loaded our luggage onto two double-decker carts and were pushing them down the hallway when I felt another rush of adrenaline. The exit sign pointed straight ahead. A few more feet and the automatic doors flew open. I felt like we had stepped into another world.

In a split second, Charlie and I went from the comfort of cool air conditioning to a solid wall of heat where the high humidity had turned the atmosphere into a giant sauna. It took a minute for us to acclimate before we joined the switchback line of people waiting for a taxi. They were so noisy, so animated, so different than the people of Eastern Europe.

The line moved quickly. When it was our turn a wiry, sprightly Chinese cabby stopped directly in front of us, jumped out, loaded our bags, glanced at the address of the hotel that Charlie showed him then whisked us away.

Riding with him was a hair raising, thrilling experience as we watched the speedometer reach ninety kilometers (55 mph) on the city streets. I wondered why I worried about a plane crash. Cars, trucks and buses piloted by aspiring kamikazes darted from lane to lane pursuing their destinations amidst a cacophony of sounds. After a few miles I promised to consider buying more life insurance if we ever made another trip for the mission.

Finally, when the driver came to an abrupt stop in front of the YMCA, we were grateful to be physically intact. A bellman was already waiting at the curb to help us. *Now this is more like the vacation I envisioned* I thought and then felt guilty.

As we stepped inside the comfortable, nicely, decorated lobby, I immediately discerned that something was missing. It was the gloom and doom that accompanied us for the last ten days. The almost tangible oppression of people, places, the despair of life itself was conspicuous by its absence. Freedom made the remarkable difference.

Without wasting any time we registered, picked up our key and followed the bellhop and our luggage into the elevator. As we approached our room on the fourth floor, the phone was ringing.

"Hurry," Charlie said to the bellhop who quickly opened the door and I rushed in to answer it. "Hello," I said swiftly.

"May I speak with either Alyce or Charles, please?" It was a woman's voice and I suspected it was our contact.

"This is Alyce, is this Sharon?" I asked.

"Yes," she answered. "I trust you had a good flight?"

"It was fine, a bit bumpy in the beginning, but..." there was no point in describing the details.

"Do you have the address and instructions to my flat?" she asked.

"Charlie does. What time would you like us be there?"

"Hold on, please," she paused and left the line for a second. "If you leave now, that will be perfect," she said when she returned.

"We're on our way."

Charlie located the instructions hidden underneath the flap in his billfold. We were ready to leave except for the most important thing; we needed to pray. A formidable task lay ahead and this was not the time to be presumptuous about

God's protection. So, with humble hearts and contrite spirits
we slipped to our knees to worship the God of situation and
circumstance. Together, we strengthened our grip on His
unseen hand.

Charlie and I sensed a renewed excitement when we
ventured into the streets of Hong Kong. The towering sky-
scrapers, banks, boutiques, shopping emporiums, expensive
restaurants and elegant hotels reminded us a little of downtown
Manhattan. Movement was everywhere: a rapid, pulsating,
exciting tempo. Limitless wealth and grinding poverty shared
the same few miles. Breathtaking beauty rubbed shoulders with
sickening squalor while noble families lived next to desperate
refugees. Hong Kong's suicide rate was one of the highest in
the world. Like Amsterdam it presented a limitless field of
opportunity for Christ's disciples. We experienced our first
taste of Asia and everything about it was overwhelming.

After walking quite a distance we decided to end our
sightseeing tour and boarded the subway at Mong Kok. The
station was crowded, but for that matter, everywhere we had
been so far was crowded so it came as no real surprise. Charlie
pushed his way inside one of the cars when it jerked to a stop
and I squeezed myself in beside him. I looked around at the
other passengers, almost all young adults.

Fortunately, we were only going a few stops and after
transferring once we arrived at the Admiralty Station on the
island side of the bay. When we stepped into the glaring sunlight
Charlie and I recognized a familiar red and white sign. A
Kentucky Fried Chicken was only three blocks from Sharon's
office.

Within five minutes, we located the building where Charlie
checked the names above the mailboxes. We were in the right
place and rode the elevator up. We stepped out on the third
floor and an indistinguishable woman standing at the end of the

dimly lit, hot, sultry hall signaled to us. When we reached the apartment we introduced ourselves to Sharon Smith.

Sharon surprised us by being an attractive woman, beautiful enough to be a fashion model. Her simple, cotton paisley dress gave her the carefree appearance of a California beachcomber. There was no question in my mind that she looked out of place in her dismal setting and miscast as a conspirator in a clandestine operation. I smiled inwardly knowing there could be only one reason for Sharon to be working in Hong Kong under these precarious conditions. His name was Jesus.

A noisy window air conditioner blew a very welcomed cool breeze across the small room filled with some old furniture that barely left enough room to walk. The kitchen was the size of an American walk-in closet and the stove and refrigerator were smaller than any I had ever seen before. In spite of the cramped quarters, everything was neat. On the wall hung a picture of Christ with Moses and Abraham. After spotting it I immediately felt right at home knowing we shared a common love for the Lord.

Sharon invited us to sit at the table; it was time to get down to business. "Did you have any trouble getting here?" she asked.

"No, your directions were very good," Charlie answered.

"May I offer you something to drink before we start? Coffee? Coke?"

We both said "No."

Sharon sat across from us and began sorting through some documents. I watched her and something about the setting and the moment reminded me of John's office in Zwolle. Finally, she found whatever she was looking for and began our orientation.

"You will travel to the mainland by boat," she said narrowing her green eyes. "We feel it is by far the safest way for you to enter right now under the circumstances." She, of course, was referring to the political fallout from the recent Tiananmen Square Massacre.

"How tight are the borders?" I asked.

"We're not sure. We have very limited information but we do know that the entire country is tense. All our deliveries stopped when the confrontation began. You will be the first ones to go in since the massacre. You must be very, very careful, very discreet. No one, absolutely no one must suspect what you are there to do."

She scrutinized us carefully, perhaps trying to judge our commitment, our courage, our effectiveness. I appreciated her honesty. At least, I think I did. Charlie flashed me his timely "don't worry, be happy" look and I feigned a smile in response. For his sake, I tried to calm my impatience to know everything that was going on and what will happen.

Someone knocked gently on the door and Sharon left us to answer it. While we waited, we heard muffled voices out in the hall. She returned and said, "The visa man is here to pick up your photographs and passports."

I dug through my purse, handed them to her and she disappeared again. This time when she returned she was not alone. A handsome young Chinese couple were with her.

"Charles and Alyce, meet Timothy and Rebecca, your contacts in China."

Charlie stood, we both smiled and said "Hello."

Our contacts? I thought. If Sharon was an unlikely candidate for her job, these two were amazing. Radiant Rebecca and handsome Timothy looked more like perfectly groomed American yuppies than like Bible smugglers. I tried not to stare but I couldn't help admiring them knowing what their involvement meant. Breaking the law in China was risky business for the Hong Kong Chinese. The authorities treated them like traitors and were especially brutal to those they caught. I cringed when

I considered the potential consequences of their dedication: beatings, torture, imprisonment, execution and all at the cruel hands of their own people.

When Rebecca and Timothy joined us at the table, Sharon's orientation resumed. Charlie and I leaned over to study the hand drawn map. "Here is the Guangzhou Terminal," Sharon said pointing. "Charles and Alyce, you will enter here then go to this area for a luggage cart. Strap your bags securely with several straps. Tie them, twist them, knot them."

She glanced up to see if we were paying close attention. We were, definitely. Sharon continued. "Sometimes having to untangle such a maze of knots discourages an agent from a search. Who knows, you might get through without any problem."

I gave Sharon a hopeful look. She responded with, "I said sometimes. Act innocent remember you are a tourist visiting China on holiday."

We spent the rest of the afternoon exhausting every possible question until at last we all became very quiet. Sharon pushed the documents aside, opened her Bible and began reading from the Book of Matthew. Her voice and her words were comforting: "If two of you shall agree on earth as touching any thing they shall ask, it shall be done for them of my Father which is in heaven."

When she finished, we held hands and prayed. It was a humbling moment. I considered it a privilege to serve Jesus alongside these courageous saints.

When our prayer time ended Rebecca and Timothy left giving us big smiles and three slight bows from the waist. We would meet again soon but what would happen between now and then was anyone's guess.

I had little time for speculation because we had so much to do. Sharon led us to the narrow bedroom where a white plastic shade silhouetted the iron bars outside the window. Stacks of luggage and literature set on the bed, the floors, everywhere and she pointed to the soft blue bags inside the open closet. They were a little larger than the small duffel bags people used at the gym but the same type.

"Heavy," Charlie groaned as he pulled them out for her.

"You bet," she replied.

"Here, let me see," I said.

I stood between them, grasped the padded cloth handles using both hands and lifted.

"You're right, they are heavy," I said after setting them down quickly. Sharon was watching me closely, so I added, "But I'll manage."

"Are sure you'll be all right?" she asked me. I sensed her concern. "You know that we will be praying and asking our Lord to keep you from harm."

"Yes, I know." I smiled, to imitate her calm and confidence on the outside while inside I worried. This time, we had no camouflage, no Baby Blue with her hidden compartments nor did we have the advantage of a political system in the midst of positive change. No, this time it was us, the border guards and God.

We gave Sharon a key to our hotel room so that someone could drop off the luggage for us since the bags were too heavy to manage on the crowded subway. Now it was time to leave and the Hong Kong sky looked gray when we stepped outside. Charlie's somber expression told me exactly how he felt and I wasn't feeling much better myself. The busy streets had me in a daze as we walked to the Admiralty station.

On the way we passed a man hawking for business who handed me what I supposed to be another advertisement. I took it even though at the time I wasn't exactly interested in buying another watch or having a tailor make a new suit. I stuffed it into my purse to read later, maybe.

Suddenly, Charlie pointed to a mannequin in a clothing store. "Chop, look at that."

We stopped and stared at the lifeless form wearing a white tee shirt with a startling message in bold black letters:

MESSAGE FROM GOD—DON'T TRUST THE GOVERNMENT.

"That's not good news," I said.

Charlie said nothing but we walked slowly after that; I suppose because we were both thinking about the future.

Our agenda sounded like a plot for a spy novel and Charlie's position at the naval base at home had only complicated the issue. Earlier a VIP from Naval Intelligence warned him about the difficulties with his security clearance. If we had trouble with the Chinese government, it would be our problem not the Navy's. He made his position very clear since the United States had no relations with Red China at the time.

Our ride back to the hotel seemed to drag. By the time we went upstairs to our room, the four bags were already inside. Charlie stepped over them and clicked on the television to catch the news. Every channel carried further appalling reports and speculation on the two day old massacre in Tiananmen Square. Questions remained unanswered: What happened? How many were killed? And why? The spokesman for the People's Republic denied most of the allegations. We did not know what to believe.

It was nightfall before we finally finished sorting through the items to leave behind and repacked our clothing around the Bibles. We stretched out on the bed not in the mood to do much of anything.

Charlie read to me from the book of Hebrews before we prayed. The clock on the night stand beside the bed read only 9:35 when we ended our devotions. But there was one thing we were constantly confronting called jet lag. Admittedly, it wasn't that late but we decided to try to go to sleep anyway certain that tomorrow would be another eventful day.

I fully expected another restless night and Charlie did too. When neither of us opened our eyes again until the next morning it came as quite a surprise. We showered quickly, then paused to check the weather before deciding what to wear. The spotty clouds from the day before were vying with the sunshine meaning the weather could go either way.

After some indecision, I chose my touristy, emerald green pantsuit and had to struggle with the defiant zipper. Everything else was ready from the night before so we left as soon as we finished dressing.

Downstairs, the bellman responsible for our stored luggage handed Charlie the receipts. We walked outside to watch for the man who would bring us our visas and return our passports. We were ready to leave the minute he arrived.

I waited until it started to drizzle before heading inside. Charlie braved the mist and remained on the sidewalk lingering under the canopy to stay dry. The lobby was empty so I made myself comfortable on the couch near the front desk. I purposely sat facing the window to watch the door and also listen for any incoming calls.

The quiet moment gave me a few minutes to think. It was still difficult to grasp the reality of being in Asia. Obviously, the life of a normal Christian was full of surprises because a visit to Hong Kong had never occurred to me. Not for any reason, much less the one we had come to pursue.

My thoughts continued to drift as the unique sounds of oriental music floated through the room. Then my eyes drifted downward remembering the dreadful legacy that had taken us around the world to Red China.

The year was 1949 when Mao Tse Tung seized power from

the dictator Chiang Kai-shek. Mao started the bloody Cultural Revolution soon after, intending to purge China of Christianity and her intelligentsia. The Communist Party then closed the door to the outside world convinced they had accomplished the goal. Only a small body of believers remained and they were isolated, detached and forgotten by Christians in the west until eventually they disappeared from the history books.

Only by God's grace, they endured. The remnant held to their beliefs and prayed for revival until they multiplied into hundreds then thousands. They met secretly in homes hidden from the despotic eyes of the Public Security Police. Even beyond the reach of the government's controlled "Three Self Church."

How many faithful represented China's underground church?

Estimates claimed fifty million, maybe more while the numbers continued to swell. The Holy Spirit harvest appeared unstoppable and continued to unnerve the godless leaders of China.

They begged for Bibles, for training and teaching materials. The need was tremendous and the task of meeting it staggering. And God was watching. What a glorious opportunity awaited Christians in the free world to minister to the spiritual hunger of China's converts. Who were Charlie and I that we should play a small part in His wonderful plan?

"Alyce!" the sharp tone of Charlie's frantic voice startled me back to reality. "I don't understand what's going on. It's already 9:30 and there's no sign of the visa man. We had to leave fifteen minutes ago to make the deadline, but he's not even here yet."

Charlie's reaction was reasonable only I didn't know what to do either and before I could say anything he started walking away. "Listen there's a telephone down the hall. I'm going to call Sharon and tell her the delivery man never showed up."

"Okay," I answered and stood. I checked at the front desk in case he had called.

When Charlie returned he didn't have to tell me what happened, his expression said it all. "No answer, right?"

"Right! Nobody's home."

"There are no messages here either."

Charlie checked his watch against the wall clock: 9:45. "If he doesn't show within the next five minutes we won't make it through the heavy traffic."

"God, please, just one more miracle," I whispered.

The prayer slipped from my lips as a Chinese man clasping a briefcase to his side rushed over. "Friends of Sharon?" We nodded our heads. "So sorry, so sorry to be late. Dreadful time getting here. See, have passports and visas."

He waved the paperwork at us. Charlie took it. "Aren't we too late?" He asked swiftly, "the boat leaves in fifteen minutes."

"Must hurry. My car out front. I drive you to pier. Hurry!"

I prayed keeping my eyes halfway closed on the hair raising tear down Nathan Road. When we reached the waterfront the frantic little man screeched to a stop at the deserted dock and we climbed out of his car stopping only to glance at the two towering ships moored there. One of them had to be ours and I could hardly wait. They appeared to me as dramatic and mysterious as the Orient herself.

With only four minutes left to board we grabbed our stuff and ran toward the vacant terminal. When we reached the boarding area we were faced with a zigzag of metal partitions suitable as an obstacle course in an athletic competition. There was no short cut to the beginning so we had to start at the end and race up one, down the other, up, down, up, down, trying to cut curves to save steps.

Charlie reached the gate first. "It's locked," he sputtered.

By then we were both out of breath and panting. "Oh no," I moaned, "now what do we do?"

"Climb over, what else."

Frantically, he began slinging our bags to the other side where they landed with a thud. Then he reached for me. "You're next, I'll help you."

"But Charlie . . . what will I do if my pantsuit rips . . ." I hesitated but he insisted.

"Come on, we have to hurry."

I knew better than to resist. Carefully, I threw my leg up to mount the rail and straddled it for a split second before Charlie shoved me over. I was just getting up when he lowered himself next to me. We grabbed our bags and took off again running. *If only they weren't so heavy,* I groaned silently.

Seconds later we stood at the immigration desk. Only a few officers were lingering around and I wondered if that was good or bad. We zipped through then followed the signs down to Pier 6. A crewman standing beside the gangplank took our tickets and helped us with the heavy suitcases.

We darted up the steep, rocking, wooden ramp as it creaked under our weight and I kept a tight grip on the railing to steady myself . The deafening sound of the air horns blared twice signaling our departure. Glancing up I saw the menacing "hammer and sickle" emblem on both smoke stacks. Suddenly I felt very small.

Father God, solely by Your grace are we able to enter behind the Bamboo Curtain and accomplish Your will.

9
China,
The Land Beyond

Charlie and I reached the main deck of the old cruise ship, the Red Star, and stopped abruptly when we saw all the commotion. Chatty Chinese people were everywhere stirring above and below us, coming, going, standing, sitting, just moving and milling around. Life among the masses was still somewhat of a culture shock for me; bedlam was the word I decided most precisely described the scene. We weren't quite sure what to do next until a young couple deserted their place at the guard rail and we hurried over to claim the spot before anyone else did.

Minutes later the captain announced our departure again by blaring the air horns several more times and I covered my ears to muffle the deafening sound. Now, we were underway. The huge white hull sliced through the water leaving deep trenches with splashing ripples scurrying in its wake. Today, it would take us on a journey up the Pearl River and into mainland China making its first stop at Guangzhou.

From where we were standing I couldn't see much of the ship's exterior but I did notice the deep orange rust stains and spots of half eaten through metal. To me, the entire vessel looked in dire need of repair, either that or a complete overhaul including the rumbling engine. But regardless of its poor condition I also thought it was intriguing, almost legendary — a replica from the days of the Opium War reminiscent of slight little men with dark secretive slanted eyes and clouds of white smoke. I wasn't really much of a history student so I'm not sure how accurate my impressions were but it was fun to let my imagination loose. One thing was for sure, however, it looked more romantic at a distance than it did close up.

The bay itself was an oily, smelly mass of putrid water spotted with floating debris and bobbing trash, stained by a mixture of gasoline and human pollution. *The Orient,* I thought to myself, *why do I found it all so captivating?* I couldn't imagine.

When it started drizzling, I turned my face to the heavens. The gentle drops felt clean, cool, refreshing like a soothing balm they trickled across my cheeks. I took a deep breath; the moist air smelled wonderful and helped to clear my head and calm my nerves.

Most of the other passengers ran for cover while we decided to stay put to capture our first glimpses of Hong Kong from the harbor with all the exotic sights and sounds surrounding us: sampans, yachts, junks, hydrofoils, ferries and freighters, each navigated the bustling waterway creating a maze of movement. The mind-boggling scene reminded me of a busy city intersection with the traffic lights out. Who was directing traffic? I don't know. And how they kept from running into each other I will never understand.

The drops were beginning to come down harder which suggested the rain probably wouldn't stop anytime soon. We certainly didn't want to miss this once in a lifetime opportunity but admittedly our clothing was becoming thoroughly soaked. Charlie wiped the water from his face with his handkerchief. When he wrung it out, we knew it was time to leave and seek shelter with the other passengers.

Charlie held my arm to steady me while we walked across what had become a slippery deck until we finally reached the main entrance to the restaurant. I ran my fingers through my hair trying to fluff up the soggy ends as we entered, a futile effort.

Once inside, we peered through the thick cigarette smoke and stopped to listen to the unintelligible chatter, wondering if we were missing out on something exciting about to happen.

For us to find seats appeared to be an impossibility until two older men wearing Mao suits unexpectedly vacated their places at a table for three. Charlie and I hustled over and sat down; the one remaining Chinese man sat across from me.

When the stranger looked up from his meal our eyes met. His professional appearance reminded me a little of my brother minus the black hair and slanted eyes. I guessed that he was Hong Kong Chinese. Since I had already adopted the custom of nodding and smiling I returned his gesture immediately. He struck me as approachable so this time I took the initiative to introduce ourselves.

"Hello. What's your name?" I asked him with a lilt in my voice.

"Jimmy Fan," his answered politely.

"Nice to meet you, Jimmy. I'm Alyce and this is my husband, Charlie." I asked him the next question just to get a conversation started. "Do you live in Hong Kong?"

"Yes," he replied still smiling, "with my family."

Something about Jimmy's manner convinced me that he was definitely the friendly type and I was elated about the prospect of speaking with a local. Charlie gave me his "slow down Alyce" look because he knew how eager I was to learn everything about life in Hong Kong. I had so many questions that needed answers. What were people saying about the Tiananmen Square Massacre? What did he think about Hong Kong's return to Chinese control in 1997? Would the situation lead to an upheaval that spelled disaster for the people living in the small British Colony? What was the Chinese point of view?

At precisely the same moment our waitress appeared. She looked at us wearing a wry little smile which made me think she spoke little or no English. Charlie discreetly pointed to Jimmy

Fan's plate signifying he would have the same. The dish resembled chicken fricassee minus the chicken and I considered ordering it for a moment. Then she put her hand on her hip and her impatient gesture warned me to make up my mind without asking questions so I decided to have a bowl of plain white rice instead.

She left and I returned to my interview with Jimmy Fan. "Have you made any personal plans for 1997 when the communists take over?" I asked him and then felt awkward because maybe I was taking advantage of his good nature by questioning him about such a sensitive subject.

To my relief, he answered without the slightest hesitation. "Yes, we have made plans. My wife and I are moving to Canada with our three children before it happens."

"Really, it sounds like you have quite a challenge ahead of you. Are you looking forward to moving?"

"No, I'm not. Hong Kong is our home, the only home we have ever known and we're happy here. The prospect of leaving it has been difficult for us to deal with. Yet I know that if we stay until the tanks come down from Beijing it will be too late. Then the authorities will do whatever they want, they will have us trapped." He paused then looked me directly in the eye. "How would you feel if you had to leave America because it was being taken over by a hostile government?"

"Hm," I said and broke eye contact. "That's difficult to answer, Jimmy. I don't know and thank God I've never had to think about it."

I felt sure that Jimmy was a patriot and if not a patriot than certainly a good citizen of his country just as I was of mine. And what I hesitated to say was that I'm an American and I always want to be an American. Instead I changed the subject.

Jimmy Fan graciously answered all my other questions about the current political situation only I dared not ask the most important one. Did he know Jesus Christ as his personal

Savior? It was obviously not the proper time nor the place and might cause trouble for everyone. Wisely, I planted the only seed possible under the circumstances and chose my words carefully. "Remember Jimmy, life may not always be fair but God is always good."

For a moment, he held me with his eyes. Did he want to know more? If so, he would ask the right person at the right time; God Himself would see to that.

Our waitress brought the food and Charlie dove in. Plain rice is boring but I was hungry and the soy with a dash of pepper made it tasty.

Jimmy asked Charlie. "Have you been to China before?"

"No, this is our first trip."

"Perhaps, you would like to read a letter from one of my friends who attends school in Fujian Province? It may help you understand the students' motives for their demonstration in Tiananmen Square a little better."

"Sure I would," Charlie quickly responded and Jimmy dug into the small black pouch tied to his slender waist. He took out the letter, unfolded it and handed it to him.

"Read it aloud," I prompted Charlie who pushed his empty plate to the side, cleared his throat and began:

I am writing you from my fifth floor dorm room at the University which has 7,000 students on campus. Our tiny window overlooks the Sea of China. Crumbled plaster with rust and mold are all over. Our bathroom floor is a constant puddle of leaky plumbing. Roach droppings are everywhere. The building we live in is located in a humid, Asian style ghetto. There is clamor, shouting and door slamming where people stare at us as we climb the five floors to our room to sleep on our tiny hard beds. We do our laundry in a bucket. At meals we pick out cockroach legs, dead flies, snails, chicken feet, veins and dozens of bone chips. We're sick of the food and the classes are very hard. There is never any hot water. People shout at each other on buses and the stench of urine and sewage is everywhere. Ours is a filthy land but awesome and ancient. I am now uncertain whether I will stay on or return home to Hong Kong.

Charlie finished reading, refolded the letter into its original creases and returned it to Jimmy. We were deeply moved, hardly able to imagine such dreadful conditions, especially in a college dorm. "That's a real eye opener, thanks for letting me read . . ."

I screamed, pointing to a crack between the floor boards. "A rat!" I recoiled in horror at the twitching whiskers, the pointed teeth and the beady eyes peering up at us from the dark.

Startled, both men looked over at me and Charlie said calmly, "Chop, it's probably only a mouse and rodents aboard ship are part of the decor."

"No, you're wrong. It's a rat. I know it is," I insisted.

"Oh, for Pete's sake," Charlie shook his head and shrugged while Jimmy laughed. "Okay have it your way but by now the unlucky rat is gone and still running from you in terror."

I shuddered. "Well, that's easy for you to say since crawling creatures don't bother you the way they do me."

After a moment of quiet Jimmy stood. "If you will excuse me," he said politely, "I must go." He slid his chair neatly under the table and disappeared down the stairs.

In view of the new addition to the neighborhood I was also ready to leave. I had hoped we could return to our original spot on the deck but when Charlie opened the door part way and we peeked outside we could see that the weather had taken a turn for the worse. The rain was now falling in torrents. The gentle rolling waves that had escorted us up the river were quickly becoming piles of water and the black lowering sky threatened us with a rough trip ahead.

Charlie had to push hard against the blistering wind to shut the door. Since the upper deck was out of the question we decided to go below instead. When I spotted a ladies' room at the bottom of the steps I went over to wait in line behind a young Chinese mother holding a baby over her right shoulder. The child's angelic, cupie doll face was only inches from mine. Whether it was a boy or girl, I couldn't tell. Her mother turned around when I made a clucking noise hoping to encourage a smile. Then I noticed something unusual. The baby had a long slit down the rear of her pants exposing her bare buttock. No diapers in China? How risky, enough said.

Eventually, it was my turn. Even though the pungent stench of ammonia from the urine burned my lungs, I went inside holding my breath as long as I could. Since there were no doors, I ducked into the rear stall for some privacy but when I spotted the infamous "squat," I froze. Straddling a hole in the floor left a lot to be desired. *I'm not ready for this,* I lamented and decided I would try again later perhaps.

I went to find my husband wondering if his experience was similar to mine. It was and he was already waiting for me. After a few minutes of discussion we agreed it would be better for us to return to the first deck where we found an empty spot along the wall. It made a nifty backrest so we sprawled out and made ourselves as comfortable as we could on the hard floor. We still had a long way to go.

The storm showed no signs of letting up and I watched the havoc it was causing through the opposite window. One minute, the bow pointed directly into heaven and the next minute stared down into the murky deep. Then a crack of lightening followed by a loud rumble of thunder made me flinch. Fortunately, miraculously, my stomach kept under control during all the violent movement. Hours later, when we finally reached our destination I didn't care if I ever boarded another Chinese boat.

We watched as the crew secured the lines and lowered the gangplank. Charlie and I joined the crowd inching their way to the terminal. I tried to imagine being one of the Cambodian Boat People, a refugee who finally reaches land having absolutely nothing but hope. *Hope in what? Without Christ there is no hope. Even so, wasn't I a wanderer too with my citizenship in heaven? Yes, maybe in some ways we're all refugees, only theirs is a life of desperation without the Savior or his precious word which I possessed. I must never take it for granted.*

When we came to a standstill, I hoped Charlie and I were inconspicuous. I looked around at the people to my left, right, behind and in front. My blond hair and blue eyes were alone in a sea of black scalps and Charlie towered over everyone by almost a foot. Not another Caucasian face was visible. How wonderfully we both stood out. God had a peculiar sense of humor if he thought we could cross this border without being noticeable.

The slow moving mob formed a dragon's tail, thick at the top narrowing when it reached ground level. Police and customs agents were everywhere and the sight of their drab olive uniforms, red arm bands and hard hats with five-pointed stars made me nervous. Once again, I sensed the familiar atmosphere of intimidation, hate, cruelty and evil. It made my skin crawl.

Eventually, we reached the terminal that was nothing more than a huge metal building. Charlie left me in the middle of a whirlpool of activity while he elbowed his way through the hordes of people to retrieve our suitcases. In keeping with the plan, I scanned the area searching for a luggage cart. I had pinned my hopes to Sharon's statement about a cart being an extremely helpful accomplice. My eyes studied every corner carefully without success. There were none anywhere and I was beginning to panic.

Charlie returned with two of our bags and dropped them at my feet. I looked up at him and said nervously "Charlie I don't see any carts anywhere."

His eyes darted from one corner to the other while he asked.

"None? Are you sure?"

"Yes, I'm sure." I said swiftly. "Oh Charles, I'm afraid this is not a good sign." This time he made a slow circle while his eyes searched the entire area.

"See what I mean, nothing," I said when he turned back to face me.

"You're right. But I don't know what I can do about it at the moment. Suppose you stay here and pray while I go find the other bags; at least that way we'll have them all together. Perhaps, they've slung them through the window by now."

"Are you for real, through the window?"

"Literally." He answered.

Charlie hurried off leaving me to grapple with my fears. I knew I had to come to terms with what I believed once and for all. Either Jesus was in control of my life or He wasn't and I was on my own. After a few moments of prayer, I squared off against my will determined to follow wherever He might lead while holding onto His unseen hand.

While I was busy wrestling with my humanity, God was busy answering my prayer because suddenly, a gust of wind blew the door behind me open. When I felt the curtains brush against my left side I spun around to see what was happening. At that instant, a luggage cart came rolling through the opening catapulting itself into the back of my leg. I stood there for a second stunned. After I came to my senses, I dove for the handle. Everyone nearby stared at me as I defended my position behind the only hand trolley in the entire terminal and clung desperately to this miraculous sign of divine intervention.

When Charlie returned with the rest of the bags, we placed them on the cart and secured them by using the multiple straps as Sharon had instructed tangling them every which way. Having done that, my hopes soared temporarily.

Immigration was next and we pushed our cart loaded down with material slowly over to one of the tables to collect the necessary paperwork. I huddled together with Charlie reading over the form when we realized that now we had a new problem. A serious one.

Filling out the health form was a snap but the customs declaration was the problem. The money section was clear-cut and simple: We didn't have much left. Only the box for declaring printed matter was another issue. No matter how we looked at it, Bibles were "printed matter." Do we check yes or do we check no? Checking "Yes" could mean immediate trouble; checking "No" could mean immediate big trouble.

Then something struck me as odd and I whispered my observations to Charlie. "You know what? This is ironic. If only the authorities here would legalize deliveries we wouldn't have to go through all this. It would make everyone's life so much easier. Why do they insist upon categorizing the Bible as pornography or as if it contained some mysterious power?"

Charlie nodded his agreement. "I know, it's crazy. At home, in a supposedly Christian nation where the Bible is accessible people argue over its relevancy and ignore God. Here, the atheists fear a Book about a God whose existence they deny. Mixed up world we live in, isn't it."

I sighed deeply and shook my head in disgust. "Anyway, so what are we going to do about their inquisitive little form?"

"Listen, I have an idea," Charlie said. "Why don't we leave it blank and maybe they'll overlook it."

I leaned a little closer and lowered my voice. "Charlie, are you serious?"

"Yes. What else can we do, we can't lie and why make their job easy." I didn't answer because I was thinking it over. Charlie's idea made sense, a long shot but . . . .

While we deliberated the large crowd dwindled. After agreeing that leaving the space empty was our best if not our only option, we stepped back in line. We kept moving. When it was our turn to face the guard in the booth, I smiled and handed him our documents. He took it without changing his expression.

I held my breath then turned sideways and flashed Charlie a worried look before turning back. The guard kept staring at the form as if it were a blank piece of paper. We waited . . . and waited . . . and waited. Time seemed to stand still and I wondered if he was blind or maybe he didn't know how to read?

Finally, he separated the two sheets, put the top copy in a drawer then pushed the other one toward me.

I smiled stifling a nervous giggle, trying not to act relieved. I picked up our copy and turned back to Charlie. "Whew," I said under my breath. Charlie shifted his eyes back and forth to remind me that we were still being watched so I took the hint and started walking away. If only I had not been too obvious.

We followed the next line into a narrow room where the process had slowed and the hubbub started all over again. I peered around the man standing in front of me to see what was going on. When I did I cringed and thought I would die of heart failure.

A large x-ray machine stood against the wall in full operation. With my hopes sinking fast, I checked out the rest of the room. On the other side in the hand search area, a young forlorn couple watched pathetically as a female officer carelessly dumped out the contents of their plastic bags that doubled for luggage on the counter. I wondered what she hoped to find and if she did find it what would become of them. Never mind them! What would become of Charlie and me if they found our Bibles? The next twenty minutes would tell.

We moved up a few more feet and waited patiently for the people ahead of us to place all their belongings on the moving belt. Since they still had several articles to go I turned around hoping that my husband might be of some encouragement but his face was white and his eyes were glazed over. I don't even know if he realized I was still there. I frowned. Evidently, I must search elsewhere for my courage.

Our turn came to confront the guard who controlled the flow of traffic. He had positioned himself in the center of the aisle but instead of following the simple procedure, I froze. *Don't just stand there, do something!* I said to myself but I couldn't move. I just looked at him wondering. *Why did he remind me of Goliath?* He was short not tall and his loud mouth was not shouting blasphemies. If only I had King David's faith because no one and I mean no one except maybe Mao himself would pass unless he said so.

Suddenly, he and the x-ray were all that stood between us and the world outside but there was one other problem; I had become a statue. I stared at him. He stared back and time ceased to be.

Then something unexplainable happened.

A man stepped out from behind the X-ray machine, shouted something to the guard then signaled for us to wait where we were as the belt ground to a halt. *Now what's going on?* I wondered and during that interminable moment, I recalled Sharon's final words. "Act innocent. Remember, you are a tourist visiting China on holiday." *Of course, that's what I'll do, how could I forget.* I snapped my fingers with delight and assumed my most innocent tourist visiting China facade.

Immediately, the belt began to hum again and now I had to make my move. Confident of my plan, I took a few steps forward and blessed Goliath with the sweetest American smile he had ever seen. Now to just keep smiling and walking and walking and smiling until we reached the door.

Only to my dismay instead of weakening, Goliath sneered then pointed first to our cart and back then to the machine. Only a idiot would not understand what he meant. I took a deep breath and swallowed hard. *Did this mean that my plan wasn't going to work?* That's when my breathing stopped again.

I decided to try my performance once more this time using

all the body language I could think of. So I rolled my eyes, shrugged my shoulders and clasped my hands together feigning more confusion. It didn't work either.

He glowered at my performance when my eyes said I did not have a clue about what he was demanding. Ironically, I was just getting into playing my part, the part of a confused soul when everything changed.

Without wasting another minute he started walking toward me. *Surely he wouldn't get physical?* Probably not but as far as he was concerned the fun and games were over. He was serious and now he really had me scared. And not only that but I was sure my pulse had quit only I was too afraid to faint.

Charlie who had been watching my feeble attempts decided not to prolong the inevitable. We would cooperate.

Charlie began maneuvering the cart backwards to the front of the machine. Trembling, I followed behind him until he was in position and pulled to a stop. Slowly, I bent over and rested one knee on the dirty floor watching my hand shaking terribly while I started undoing the knots. After loosening only a few I felt a steadying hand on my left shoulder. I stopped what I was doing, turned and glanced up and into the face of another guard who was motioning for us to follow him. Feeling numb, I stood and we obeyed trailing him like two lambs to the slaughter.

My imagination went wild. *Where was he taking us?* I knew the Chinese communists were notorious for making public examples of private people. *Was that it, had I guessed right? Would we be the scapegoats to send a message to the Christians to stop the steady flow of Bibles entering the country?* I didn't know what to think.

Everyone moved aside, out of our way, as we approached. Even tyrannical Goliath had his back to us when we passed by and appeared not to even notice our departure. What did they know that we didn't? It was an indescribable, unnerving experience.

The official or whoever he was walked straight ahead until we had almost reached the other end of the room very near to the exit. The traffic noise and pedestrian chatter coming from the street were within earshot. We stopped just short of the door when I turned around to see if Charlie was feeling as confused as I was about where we were headed. I questioned him with my eyes but his blank expression meant that he had no answers about what was going on either.

When I turned back the guard who had escorted us this far had disappeared. *What? Where? When? How?* I blinked and swallowed hard. I couldn't believe my eyes. One minute he was standing right there in front of me and now he was gone.

I spun around searching in every direction but there was no door, no side hallway, no obstacle big enough to conceal a grown man. He had simply vanished.

I asked Charlie. "Where's the guard? Where did he go?"

"I don't know! This is crazy! I don't know what happened because I was looking at you!"

Dumfounded by his mysterious disappearance, Charlie and I stood alone in front of the door. Nobody was even watching us and the door to the outside stood wide open.

Was it a trap? Or was it God?

10
The Final Miracle

Suddenly charged with divine energy, Charlie and I whispered simultaneously, "Let's go!"

At top speed, we undid the straps, grabbed the bags, and shoved the cart out of our way. Without looking back even once, we dashed outside, slammed our luggage into the first taxi we saw, then jumped in ourselves. We must have startled the driver when we commandeered his cab before saying anything to him. Charlie quickly handed him the address of our hotel, and he took off.

"Hurry!" I said.

"Step on it!" Charlie added.

I was still flabbergasted by our experience at customs, rehearsing it in my mind, reliving the strange emotions. *What happened? Who was that mysterious guard that led us to the exit door? Where did he come from and just as important where did he go? Had we really seen another miracle? Another angel perhaps?*

More than anything I wanted to discuss it with Charlie because I knew he must be asking himself the same questions. But I didn't dare. We could not be certain whether the driver understood English or if he was a communist cadre (officer) instructed to pretend not to. Ultimately, I concluded that yes, yes! we had seen another angel, a Chinese angel at that.

We had gone only a short distance before we were caught

in the heavy traffic on the city streets, and our driver was forced to slow down. Finally, I could relax at least for now and enjoy the warm breeze blowing though the open window that kept my hair fluttering around in circles. Guangzhou reminded me of Hong Kong only everything that went on seemed even more intense, if that were possible. The city streets were bustling, alive with movement, vibration and noise. Scads of pedestrians crowded the sidewalks, while cars jammed the pavement, and bicycles everywhere—more than I had ever seen before— jangled their jingling bells. Behind all the orderly confusion were the lives of the people, their needs, their desires and the mysterious way it all appeared to flow together, and under- neath, their desperate need to learn the Word and the will of God.

Time passed quickly. Twenty minutes later, Charlie and I stood at the registration desk of the Lily Pond Hotel, the government run hotel where we had confirmed reservations for the night. The desk clerk was tied up with a loud, lively phone conversation, and nobody else paid any attention to us. I stood there next to Charlie, daydreaming about submerging myself in a hot bath, with clean water covering my shoulders, brisk bubbles floating through my toes, and steam penetrating my pores. Wonderful, wonderful: I could hardly wait.

The desk clerk hung up the phone, then glanced up at Charlie who was holding out our room voucher. I sensed a sudden cocky attitude overtake the clerk, who declared sharply, "We have no rooms!" Either it was true, or he disliked Americans on sight.

Charlie held up the form. "You have one for us," he insisted. "See? We have a guaranteed reservation right here."

The clerk ignored the slip of paper and without changing his stoic expression shook his head and said, "No!" and turned around. Charlie and I stood there staring at his back stunned by his reaction, as he began sorting through a stack of mail. We were stumped. We waited a few more minutes to see if perhaps he might change his mind.

When it was obvious he was not going to, I decided to take the "bull by the horns," as they say, and called, "Yoo-hoo! Are you there? Can you help us, please?"

He turned back to face me mumbling something in his native tongue, still ignoring the voucher I held out to him.

I asked, "What did you say? Sorry, but I didn't hear you."

"We have no rooms!" he barked angrily, grabbed the slip of paper out of my hand, and tossed it aside. It fell on the floor and Charlie quickly bent over to retrieve it.

"Why is nothing ever eas . . ." I started to reiterate my favorite complaint on the way out but caught myself when we reached the sidewalk. A sudden realization about the situation disturbed me, something that had nothing to do with our lodging. It was the lack of respect and common courtesy. Evidently, people in general in this communist country were simply objects of scorn.

In my mind I mulled over the way communism works, deeply affecting everyone's attitudes by creating two standards: one for party members, and the other for the common folks, imposing a caste system that divided Red Chinese society into those-who-have and those-who-have-not. Socialism had gained almost total control with its deceptive doctrine that life should be easy and that government was the source of supply, that arbitrary rights superseded opportunities.

I was no expert on political science or the destruction of democracy but I had my suspicions. Communism. Socialism. Big Brother. Big Daddy. No matter what they called it, it all added up to god spelled with a little *g*.

While I contemplated the world scenario, my husband tried to solve our immediate dilemma by soliciting the help of a friendly bellman who spoke a little English. After Charlie explained the situation, the sympathetic bellman flagged down another taxi for us. He even gave the driver instructions to take us to some other hotel. Problem solved, or so we thought.

Our new driver had a heavy foot and hit the gas pedal hard, so hard that we were both thrown backwards against the seat. I studied the man behind the wheel, a chain smoker with a continuous cloud of smoke encircling his head, who kept bobbing to the rhythm of a country western tape played full blast. The twanging electric guitars were starting to give me one of those no food no rest headaches. When my frustration reached the point of no return, I begged Charlie, "Please, ask him to turn it down."

Charlie tapped him on the shoulder and conveyed my request first in English and then using sign language. Either he didn't understand or choose not to comply. Meanwhile, I prayed and suffered.

Forty-five minutes later, the paved city street had become a country road cutting across farming communes, small villages and rice paddies with water buffalo plowing the muddy soil. Another classic scene that depicted everyday life for the Chinese peasants came with every new mile. Our tour had become like flipping the pages of a National Geographic magazine.

The landscape may have been fascinating, but the roads were a nightmare. There were no guardrails separating the traffic that moved freely from lane to lane. Farm machines, ox carts, trucks, trailers, jeeps, cars, tractors, bicycles, people, dogs, ducks and flocks of sheep in abundance all passed each other jumping or dodging potholes or bottoming out without any apparent care or concern for their own safety or the other's right of way.

So far, I had intentionally shut my eyes numerous times on what was turning out to be a long journey. We were cruising at a moderate speed when without any warning our driver stopped the car in the middle of the road and turned around to face us.

"Not going to Jollee!" he declared.

"What do you suppose he means by that?" I asked Charlie.

"I can't imagine," he answered. We leaned closer to him, and the man repeated his statement again louder. "We not going to Jollee!"

I flashed Charlie a puzzled look. "Do you think he's trying to tell us that we're lost?"

Charlie shook his head in disgust. "Who knows?"

"Great! Now what are we going to do?" I moaned.

Charlie shrugged and didn't answer.

Suddenly, the driver gunned the engine and peeled rubber. Apparently, he wanted to catch up to a young woman peddling a bicycle further up the road. The taxi covered the distance quickly but when we arrived she had already left the pavement. When he slammed on the brakes, jumped out of the car and began chasing her on foot I started wondering about his sanity. It wasn't so much what he did, it was more the way he did it that worried me. "Charlie, our driver is a very erratic unpredictable individual," I quipped.

"Don't you think I know that by now?" My husband sounded irritated and I couldn't blame him.

The young woman turned off onto a narrow dirt path, and I wondered if our driver intended to get us killed by leaving us sitting in the middle of the road again. The situation was either very comical or very dangerous. At that moment, I wasn't sure which.

"Charlie, I'm homesick," I said with a sigh.

My sad remark struck him as funny and he seemed to forget all about being anxious and started laughing. At first, I was disillusioned, but when he reached the point of hysterics, I finally joined in.

"Chop," he panted, "you do know that we're at the mercy of a madman, don't you?"

"Yes," I answered wiping the tears from my eyes. "And if

that's not bad enough, we're twelve thousand miles from home, lost and almost out of money."

Charlie's turn: "A couple of foreigners who don't speak the language lugging four heavy bags stuffed with contraband that could get them imprisoned or killed. Is that what you call a cultural experience?"

By this time, we were rocking the cab with our laughter. "And why do I have the feeling that I've seen this movie before. It was called, Adventures of Baby Blue."

We were beginning to settle down until I added one more comment. "How many want to stay long enough to learn Chinese? How many want to stay long enough for the food to start agreeing with you? Charlie, can we go home soon?" That did it. My question was like putting a match to a can of gasoline and we started our laughing fit all over again. Eventually, we quit acting like a couple of lunatics and returned to semi-normal. "Seriously," I said, "I'm glad our meeting with Rebecca and Timothy isn't until tomorrow morning. Maybe by then everything will look rosy."

When our driver returned, we noticed his new sense of confidence. He sat behind the steering wheel happily chattering in the unintelligible vernacular. Charlie gave him an encouraging pat on the shoulder as we pulled away and the tires squealed.

A short while later, our thrilling adventure with the cabby ended when he turned off the main highway and headed down a single lane unpaved road. Our destination must be close. Charlie checked his watch to verify the driving time, one hour and seven minutes. That meant we would have to leave the next morning by 7:30 to keep our appointment with Timothy and Rebecca. Nothing, absolutely nothing must jeopardize our rendezvous.

At last, a five-story brick building appeared out of the dust-colored sky, the Jollee Hotel, an experience we will never forget. The bright sign out front with most of its bulbs missing resembled the toothless smile of a vagrant, while its dim yellow light cast a foreboding shadow over what lie ahead.

Darkness had almost smothered the last hour of dusk when our cabby dropped us off and pulled away leaving us staring at our dreary new hotel. The winding path leading to the main entrance cut through the overgrown weeds and bushes that obscured the outer limits to the property. Its eerie appearance reminded me of a haunted house.

"Charlie," I whispered and tried to be funny, "where's the rising fog and the howl of the werewolves?" I made a stupid face and continued. "Will a black draped woman with a hooked nose and hairy warts greet us after the door screeches open by itself?"

My sense of humor obviously lacked something, good timing perhaps? Anyway, Charlie ignored me, picked up most of our luggage, and started traipsing toward the entrance. I picked up the rest and followed him. The closer we came, the worse it looked. A downstairs broken window still had several pieces of splintered glass sticking out of the frame. No telling how long it had been that way. Some vacation!

When we reached the door and stepped inside the lobby I wasn't surprised that it complemented the depressing atmosphere outside: dark, dingy, depressing in its own right. An elderly Chinese man, manning the registration desk sat still enough to be on display in a museum. We were not even sure whether his eyes were open. He wore a grayed, frayed, sleeveless undershirt and had a few long, unruly hairs hanging from his chin.

Charlie placed our voucher on the counter directly in front of him—under his nose, so to speak—to try to break his trance. It almost worked. With a minimum of motion, he reached underneath the counter for a key, laid it on top of the paper and pointed to the stairs.

"I suppose he means we go in that direction," I remarked and started to walk away.

"Wait a minute," Charlie said, then he turned to the clerk. "Don't you want us to sign in?"

The old man did not respond.

"No elevator, right?" I asked whoever.

Charlie answered. "Guess not."

I waited in the lobby while Charlie made the first trips up the stairs to our third floor room lugging some of our luggage. Together we carried the rest. By the time we reached the top landing and paused to catch our breath, an elderly Chinese woman, maybe the clerk's wife, we never did find out, emerged from a tiny room opposite the stairwell and handed us each a towel, not much bigger than a face cloth.

We followed her down the drab hallway to our room and she disappeared as Charlie opened the door. He stepped out of the way to let me go in first. I looked inside and what to my wondering eyes should appear but two little single beds, a doorless closet, a TV without a cord, a leaning lamp and a thin gauze panel masquerading as a curtain trying in vain to conceal the shamelessly bare window. And no bathroom.

No bathroom?

I plopped myself down on the nearest bed and wailed, "Charlie, no bathroom!"

"Don't worry, Chop," he said. "I think there's a ladies' room at the end of the hall near the closet lady. Didn't you smell the . . ?"

"Oh great! Community showers and squats! I can hardly wait. Now I know why the cab driver couldn't find this place. Nobody ever comes here on purpose. Why is nothing ever . . . never mind."

"Cheer up!" Charlie said encouragingly. "We can survive one night."

"Okay," I sighed. "Someday we'll get to go back home. Why don't we just repack the Bibles and hit the hay." I bounced on the bed. "Charlie, you won't believe this, but it feels like hay."

He simply frowned at me. "Start repacking if you want to; I have to shower first." With that he grabbed his miniature towel, and disappeared.

I stretched out across the bed and was about to doze off, when Charlie woke me up. He hadn't been gone more than five minutes. I squinted up at him, then sat up and stared at his grim expression. He was standing forlorn and dripping wet. He was obviously upset.

"What happened to you?" I asked. "What did you do to your hair? Yuk! It's sticky." I raised both my eyebrows at his greasy new look.

"Some shower!" he growled. "As soon as I soaped up the water stopped."

"You're kidding!" I could picture that happening to him and tried to squelch my giggle.

"Don't laugh! It'll probably do the same for you."

A smirk continued fighting for mastery of my face, but I tried to appear sympathetic. "Honey, why don't you go try again. Maybe the water's back on. At least rinse your hair before you come to bed."

"Okay," he said reluctantly, "but this is the last time." He hung his wet towel over the chair and grabbed mine.

After he left, I sorted out my books for delivery and slipped into my pajamas. I had just finished when he returned in a much better mood. "Well, you certainly look better. It must have worked," I commented cheerfully.

"Let's just say it worked and leave it at that," he mumbled. I dropped the subject and watched him empty the contents of his pants pockets onto the dresser—passport, comb, wallet, keys, handkerchief and a few coins.

"Charlie, we have a problem," I watched him stack the

items into neat little piles.

"A problem?" He looked over at me and continued getting ready for bed.

"Yes, what should we do with our overnight bag? We can't take it with us when we meet with Rebecca and Timothy."

"I know but don't you remember Sharon's instructions? She told us to leave it with the bellman at the Guangzhou Hilton across from the government store. I'm more concerned about getting a cab way out here by 7:30 in the morning."

"Maybe, the old fellow at the desk can help, that is if you can communicate. And I wish you Godspeed and good success 'rotsa ruck,' as they say, because you'll need it."

Charlie laughed and snorted, "Oh, you're a big help."

I might have laughed too if I hadn't spotted a giant cockroach big enough to carry a saddle skittering across the floor. I screeched, "Charlie, don't leave me! Look!"

He glanced at the six-legged varmint and made his typical nonchalant comment. "Don't worry, Chop. He won't bother you. He's harmless," he said, while his size ten shoe squashed the critter and ended the life of one of billions.

"Ugh," I groaned as a shiver ran down my spine. "Charlie, pray with me, please. I feel uneasy. I don't like this place. I know God will protect us, but so much could still go wrong and I feel as though our battles aren't over yet."

He sat next to me on the bed, held my hand and we sought the Lord together. When we finished, Charlie slipped into some clean clothes and went back downstairs to arrange for a taxi. Fortunately, I fell asleep.

The next morning, a yellow sedan parked in front of the Jollee Hotel at 7:35, and honked his horn. I waved out the window to let the driver know we were ready. We left quickly and in retrospect, the Jollee hadn't been so bad; after all, they only charged us $8-American.

We were on our way and on schedule, which meant that my predication about anticipating trouble was a needless exercise. I was never so happy about being wrong. My husband's shoulder made a good headrest, and I closed my eyes as we sped peacefully toward our rendezvous.

Halfway there, the car tilted and made a dreadful noise underneath the rear end. I withered and resisted opening my eyes. I did not want to know what it was. I just wanted it to go away. Instead, the thumping became louder and the angle of the tilt sharper. When we obviously could go no further, the driver rolled to a stop and he and Charlie climbed out.

I called to Charlie out the window. "What happened?"

"A flat," Charlie answered over his shoulder. I got out to look. The rear tire was as bald as an egg and as flat as a board.

"Figures," I mumbled as I meandered back to where the driver was searching through his trunk full of broken boxes, dirty rags and plastic sandals. When a lug wrench, jack and a balding spare tire appeared on the ground, I let out a sigh of relief. With Charlie's assistance and the Lord's help, we were on our way again within fifteen minutes. Next stop, the Guangzhou Hilton.

The taxi had hardly rolled to a stop before a dozen Chinese bellboys, dressed in brown uniforms with round hats and white gloves, and lapel name tags, rushed over to greet us. The one named William reached us first.

William spoke English and Charlie quickly arranged for him to watch for our bag for a few hours. Meanwhile, my eyes swept over the sumptuous surroundings inside. Were we still in the same country?

Teeming, brilliant flowers and lush tropical plants had turned the lobby into a profuse atrium. Splashing waterfalls, rock gardens and lily ponds stocked with fat gold and white carp helped create the delightful atmosphere. Glass elevators zipped from ground level to the upper floors while groups of guests dined like nobility beside the pools. It was elegance to the max, a veritable movie set of luxurious, world-class extravagance.

Charlie caught my attention with a wave, ending my mental respite and the few moments I had stolen to enjoy the lovely distractions. It was time to go. I walked next to him to the exit where the automatic doors flung open before us. A solid wall of heat and humidity slapped us when we stepped outside. Passing from such near utopia into such hard core reality shocked my senses, and suddenly I remembered why we had come.

When we reached the street, Charlie pointed to our destination, the tall building across the plaza. A crowded circular intersection spanned the distance between us. Several side streets came together, and all the cars crammed into one massive absence of order. With no flashing lights, no signals, and no one directing traffic, the area posed a real challenge for pedestrians. Realizing that aggression ruled, we ventured boldly into the maze of confusion.

I trailed behind my husband as he waved, flagged, darted and dashed between the vehicles. We were almost to the middle of the maelstrom, when Charlie yelled, "Watch out, Chop!" The driver of a red Datsun had suddenly changed his mind and direction without warning, and swerved toward me blindly. He evidently hadn't seen me.

Charlie lunged, pulled me out of the way, and I fell. Horns blared and brakes screamed when the red Datsun jerked to a stop inches from my right shoulder. Charlie and I were both trembling as he helped me up. "Are you okay?" he asked in a shaky voice.

"I-I-I think so. But where did he come from? I didn't see him." I exhaled hard. "Whew, that was close."

"Too close," Charlie responded as the driver gave us a contemptuous look and drove away waving his fist in the air and shouting curses that we were glad we didn't understand.

Charlie put his arm around me and I leaned into his side, trying to pull myself together after my near mishap. "Hold on to me," he said gently and hugged me. "It's not much further."

I blinked back a tear and nodded my head.

We finally reached the entrance to the crowded government store where we would meet our contacts and exchange our identical luggage. Charlie avoided passing close by the officers standing around the front steps by inching our way deeper into the crowd. But when I spotted the green uniforms out of the corner of my eye, my heart started to pound. *Don't look*, I told myself hoping to act nonchalant as we passed them by busily engaged in a lively discussion. Fortunately, they paid no attention.

Droves of noisy people roamed the dusty aisles, making it a beehive of activity. Charlie guided me toward an unobtrusive spot where we could get our bearings. I watched the people, while he kept an eye on the front door. After a few minutes, we began walking slowly toward the linen counters. We knew better than to appear like we were looking for someone, but we had to stall.

Suddenly, we spotted Rebecca and Timothy coming in through the front door, and I felt a surge of adrenaline rush through my body. At that precise moment, a clerk came over to see if we needed his help. We shook our heads, no thank you, and moved away.

Charlie maintained a comfortable distance between us and our contacts, while we all watched for the right time and place to exchange bags. Timothy and Rebecca continued meandering through the aisles as we maintained a close watch on their whereabouts. I kept reminding myself to act like a wide-eyed tourist.

So far, everything had gone smoothly according to plan. We were nearing the last stages of our purpose for being in China. Soon it would be over.

Timothy stopped to examine a watch while Rebecca inspected a few pieces of luggage. Charlie and I began a casual approach in their direction, when suddenly I saw a familiar face. *Who? Where? When?*

Then I remembered and grabbed Charlie's arm with one hand and covered my mouth with the other to muffle my alarm. "Aaagh! Charlie quick, look who's coming in our direction!"

Charlie glanced over. "Thomas Li? Oh no! What's he doing here? Has he been tailing us?" By then Charlie's face was ashen.

At that moment, Rebecca caught my eye and I quickly, discreetly shook my head, no! Her expression remained bland, making me think she had not understood my message. *Jesus, what's going on?* Not knowing what else to do, I made a complete about face with my partner following from a few steps behind. At that moment, my fear shifted and I became more afraid for our Chinese contacts than for us.

Lord Jesus, Thomas Li confused me with some of his comments, but I'm sure he isn't stupid. Why was I so careless about showing him my Bible on the plane? You know I can't undue my mistakes. What's done is done. Please help us!

Maybe I was overreacting but I distrusted Li. Paranoia or supernatural discernment? Only God knew for sure. There were so many public security officers stationed at every door, it would take him less than a minute to alert them. What then? Would they question us, follow us, search us to trap us in our blatant act of civil disobedience?

Charlie and I retreated around the corner. If Thomas Li had come to watch us, we could also watch Thomas Li. He was inspecting a camera and a clerk was making some effort to assist him. Surely, Rebecca and Timothy were experienced enough to discern the danger. They would know we were not avoiding them without reason.

Li set the camera back down on the glass showcase and started walking toward the steps leading to the second floor. Within seconds he had disappeared. If he was alone, the coast was clear. Charlie and I knew that it was time to act. We had no time to lose if we were to complete the exchange before Li showed up again.

While I waited and prayed, Charlie left to locate Rebecca and Timothy. The five minutes he was out of my sight felt like an hour. *Patience, patience,* I reminded myself until I couldn't wait any longer.

With no sign of either Charlie or the other two, I walked in the same direction he had gone praying, praying, with my eyes constantly straying over to the stairs just in case Mr. Li made another appearance. *Stop it!* I chided myself. *Trust Jesus to keep him away.* Surely, God would not fail to make good on His promise never to forsake us.

Minutes later, I spotted Timothy standing in front of a display case. There were only a few people lingering in the area, so I walked up to within a few feet of him. He looked directly at me, smiled and nodded casually. His outward calm eased my fears, and I smiled back. We both knew it was time to make our move.

Timothy put his bags down on the floor as a young sales clerk came toward me. Timothy intercepted him, talking to him in Chinese, and drew him away to the opposite end of the counter. I dropped my identical bags alongside his, turned around pretending to read the overhead signs, and almost fainted when I saw Thomas Li coming back down the stairs. A sweep of paralyzing fear held me in its clutches until I looked again, closer. This man was not Thomas Li, but someone else who closely resembled him.

Meanwhile, Timothy's conversation with the clerk continued to be lively and loud. It was now or never. When I was sure no one was watching me, I picked up Timothy's empty bags. Praise God for another miracle!

I was alone, and my few Bibles were one small step closer to the hearts that had prayed and empty hands reaching out to receive them. Now, to find Charlie and Rebecca.

As I scooted around the corner, Charlie almost bumped into me. "Where were you?" I whispered.

He smiled a wide, happy, satisfied smile. "Rebecca and I met in the men's department. Have you seen everything you wanted to see?"

I grinned back. "Yes, have you?"

"Uh huh! Shall we go?"

As I took Charlie's arm, I silently added my prayer to the many interceding for Timothy and Rebecca that God would station His protecting angels around them. I felt sure that God would answer our prayers.

We departed swiftly, caught a cab to the Hilton, picked up our bag, headed for Guangzhou station, and boarded the noon train to Hong Kong.

Mission accomplished.

The next day, while settled in our seats on the plane bound for the USA, I rummaged through my purse for something to write on when I found the paper the man on the street in Hong Kong had handed me a few days earlier. I poked Charlie's arm and said, "Honey, look at this." While I read it, he read it over my shoulder:

SOCIALIST PARTY GUIDELINES

1. Find out what the people want.
2. Promise it to them.
3. Go to work to get it for them, thereby gaining their support.

4. Overthrow the government.
5. Establish a Socialist Party dictatorship.
6. Give the people what they want — temporarily, then take it from them when the appropriate time arrives.

Lord, why did You bring this to our attention now? What, if anything, does this have do with our country? Is America's future mysteriously entwined with the suffering church because Jesus said that when one suffers we all suffer? The questions bothered me during the rest of the flight. When the Los Angeles basin finally came into view, I stared out the window at the lights below. "Charlie, look! We're almost home ... I don't remember it being so beautiful before ... I wonder ... why does it seem so different to me. Surely, nothing has changed in the short time we've been gone."

"I think we're the ones who changed, Chop. We're what's different."

I smiled. Charlie was exactly right. We were definitely changed, and would never be the same again, thank God.

It was late evening when we deplaned at Gate 8 and hurried through the terminal to the baggage claim area. America! Even the dispassionate terminal had a certain glow about it. We were home. No more contraband Bibles to deliver, no more fear of doing the Lord's will, no more looking over our shoulders to see who was watching.

A little further on, we approached a group of handsome young Navy men—groomed and polished, waiting for their connections home or back to base. As we passed I murmured, "Thank you." They gave me a peculiar look. I doubt they ever heard that from stranger.

At customs Charlie and I showed our passports with no anxiety over what might follow. "Welcome home!" the agent said. "Did you have a good trip?"

We beamed at him. "Yes!" I said, "but there's no place like

home. It's wonderful to be back."

Bobby was already waiting outside in the car to meet us. "Welcome home!" he hollered. "So many people have been asking. . ."

"I'm not surprised and we'll tell you all about it later, Bobby," I answered, wondering how we could ever describe such a life changing journey.

"They've been praying."

Charlie smiled. "Yes, we could tell."

I sat in the back seat of Bobby's car clutching my carryon containing my Bible. I studied the people still milling around the airport as he drove by. What was it that Mary, that loving Polish housekeeper, had said? They stand and walk like free people. A sudden surge of patriotism brought tears to my eyes, tears of pride in my country, tears of shame for my past apathy. Now I was fully convinced that I must pray for America like never before.

America, "one nation under God, indivisible, with liberty and justice for all."

Liberty. We must cherish it, defend it.

Justice. We must esteem it highly, uphold it boldly, and stand together honorably to hold off the unseen evil forces that would seduce our people with lies.

America, America, God shed His grace on thee, and crown thy good with brotherhood from sea to shining sea. Amen.

Those who cannot remember the past are condemned to repeat it.

George Santayana, 1905

We have been assured, Sir, in the Sacred Writings that except the Lord build the house, they labor in vain that

build it. I firmly believe this. I also believe that, without His concurring aid, we shall succeed in this political building no better than the builders of Babel.

Benjamin Franklin

Of all dispositions and habits which lead to political prosperity, religion and morality are indispensable supports. In vain would that man claim the tribute of patriotism, who should labour to subvert these great pillars of human happiness, these firmest props of the duties of men and citizens.

George Washington

It is the duty of nations, as well as of men, to own their dependence upon the overruling power of God and to recognize the sublime truth announced in the Holy Spirit and proven by all history, that those nations only are blessed whose God is the Lord.

Abraham Lincoln

Our Constitution was made only for a moral and religious people. It is wholly inadequate for the government of any other.

John Adams

If at any time I announce that a nation or kingdom is to be uprooted, torn down and destroyed, and if that nation I warned repents of its evil, then I will relent and not inflict on it the disaster I had planned.

Jeremiah 18:7-8 NIV

Afterword

We returned from China that year and started writing about our travels. Since we began five years ago, Charlie and I moved from the sunny shores of California to the piney woods of Texas. In His infinite wisdom, God picked out a lovely spot for us to enter this season of our lives.

Reflecting on the past, it amuses us to think the Lord Jesus could turn a happenstance free chicken dinner into a life changing experience for so many. Without any doubt, we do serve a sovereign God, who uses the commonplace and the ordinary to perform His work. Over the past several years it has been our privilege to see the Holy Spirit lead other Christians into supplying the need for Bibles in China. Old, young, rich and poor spent their vacations with us in His harvest fields treading the streets of Asia. This exciting prospect even compelled a special few to return year after year and the small band of believers became known as the China seven. We've watched the faithful go, grow and receive blessings as they carried out His work regardless of the obstacles.

We went, we followed and we learned. The next section elaborates this, may it stir you to consider new ideas as you pursue His life's work for yourself. Scripture says, There is no new thing under the sun (Eccl. 1:9 NIV), but sometimes we gain new insights from wrapping old truths into contemporary experiences. His power often becomes more real, fresher and alive when we see it through the eyes of others. This is our heartfelt prayer.

There appears to be no set formula to use when you

consider getting involved in a ministry, rather each of us comes in our own way at our own time. Whatever opportunity or wherever His leading, we encourage you to go for it! But remember, calm waters don't make great sailors, so expect waves. Also expect great things, accept great things!

Let Him change your life forever.

Until we meet in heaven, our blessings to you.

Ministry Ideas
to Consider

*** RISK TAKING — It is often our resistance to move beyond the safe and comfortable that keeps us from the riches of serving Jesus Christ. Yet, from Genesis to Revelation the willingness to trust God with our valuable possessions, our precious loved ones and even life itself is the silver thread that ties the saints together.

When was the last time you took a risk for the sake of the Gospel? How did it turn out and in what way did it change you?

_____

_____

_____

_____

_____

_____

_____

_____

*** WHO ME? I DON'T KNOW WHERE TO BEGIN — Yes you! He calls us all into the work. If you need some persuasion, look at the life of Jesus, and the Apostles. Anyone who loves Him serves Him. Maybe you haven't found your place because you need to ask —God delights in giving us the desires of our hearts. For everyone who asks receives; he who seeks finds;

and to him who knocks, the door will be opened. (Matt 7:8) What do you want? Jesus might be asking you that question right now.

How would you answer? Have you ever asked Jesus to reveal His plan to you? Keep asking and meditating on scripture until you can write something down.

_____

_____

_____

_____

_____

_____

_____

_____

*** I CAN'T (ACTUALLY MEANS, I WON'T) — Sometimes I think we deceive ourselves with those words Satan loves to hear. I'm sure they cause him to sneer at the excuses we invent to dodge a call from the Master. He said don't complicate the message, give to the poor, visit the sick, care for the widow and orphan, preach the Gospel, equip the saints or take a stand for righteousness.

Isn't there something you can do?

_____

_____

_____

_____

_____

_____

_____

*** WHERE'S THE BEEF? — The famous phrase coined by the hamburger giant leads us to believe that sometimes things are less than what they tell us. Not so of Jesus; He promised abundant living for those who decide to pick up their cross daily and follow Him. We are spiritually poor by choice and wrong priorities. Read over Luke 14:16-35.

Have people, places or things ever sidetracked you from God's will? Are they still holding you back?

_____

_____

_____

_____

_____

_____

_____

_____

*** DON'T BUY THE LIE AND BE CHEATED — As discouraged as we may get at times with the call of ministry, our works done in Jesus' name are the only ones that will endure until the end. The Bible says all others are merely hay, wood and stubble and will be burned. Serving Christ is the only life worth living.

Do you agree? What is your perspective? How does it line up with the Scriptures?

_____

_____

_____

_____

_____

_____

*** PROBLEMS, PROBLEMS, PROBLEMS — I don't know about you but I shudder at the prospect of trouble, big trouble, little trouble, I sigh, "Who needs it." We do! If we use our troubles to draw near to Jesus, they can raise us from the earth to the heavens without even leaving our living rooms. Or they can bring out the worst in us.

Can you list how have you benefited from past problems?

_____

_____

_____

_____

_____

_____

*** WHO IS THE ENEMY ANYWAY — The world, the flesh or the devil? It's important to understand whether you need a pistol or a missile. If it is human nature we can determine to change with God's help, should it be the world we may have to accept reality, but if it is the enemy we may use our authority as God's children, and pray and fast.

Are you facing a present challenge where one of the weapons may be effective?

_____

_____

_____

_____

_____

_____

_____

*** DON'T KID YOURSELF, IT'S VERY EXPENSIVE NOT TO SERVE — In our eyes and with our limited vision it may appear service is far too costly. We don't need more guilt, but more enthusiasm given the benefits. Remember the words of King David "Neither will I offer burnt offerings unto the LORD my God of that which doth cost me nothing." (2 Sam 24:24)

What do you believe a life of service would mean to you? Make a list of the rewards Jesus promised.

_____

_____

_____

_____

_____

_____

_____

_____

*** DON'T WAIT UNTIL IT FEELS GOOD — You will never accomplish anything for God or yourself if you wait for the flesh. Instead, make a decision now to get serious with the Savior and serve Him. Remember to take it one green light at a time. Watch for confirming signs and be sure to make time to listen, and then hold on. You will be in for some true excitement.

Can you list three biblical characters who ignored their feelings and obeyed God?

_____

_____

_____

_____

_____

_____

_____

_____

*** WARNING! — For it is by grace you have been saved, through faith and this not from yourselves, it is a gift from God — not by works, so that no one can boast. For we are God's workmanship, created in Christ Jesus to do good works, which God prepared in advance for us to do. (Eph. 2:8-10 NIV). Jesus instructed us not only to hear but also to do. He never separated the two! Read Matthew 7:21.

Are your motives for service important? Think about it.

_____

_____

_____

_____

_____

_____